1 MONTH OF FREE READING

at

www.ForgottenBooks.com

By purchasing this book you are eligible for one month membership to ForgottenBooks.com, giving you unlimited access to our entire collection of over 700,000 titles via our web site and mobile apps.

To claim your free month visit:
www.forgottenbooks.com/free914309

* Offer is valid for 45 days from date of purchase. Terms and conditions apply.

ISBN 978-0-265-94940-5
PIBN 10914309

This book is a reproduction of an important historical work. Forgotten Books uses state-of-the-art technology to digitally reconstruct the work, preserving the original format whilst repairing imperfections present in the aged copy. In rare cases, an imperfection in the original, such as a blemish or missing page, may be replicated in our edition. We do, however, repair the vast majority of imperfections successfully; any imperfections that remain are intentionally left to preserve the state of such historical works.

Forgotten Books is a registered trademark of FB &c Ltd.
Copyright © 2017 FB &c Ltd.
FB &c Ltd, Dalton House, 60 Windsor Avenue, London, SW19 2RR.
Company number 08720141. Registered in England and Wales.

For support please visit www.forgottenbooks.com

MORTUARY LAW.

BY

SIDNEY PERLEY,

OF THE MASSACHUSETTS BAR.

AUTHOR OF "THE LAW OF INTEREST," "MASSACHUSETTS ADJUDICATED FORMS," ETC.

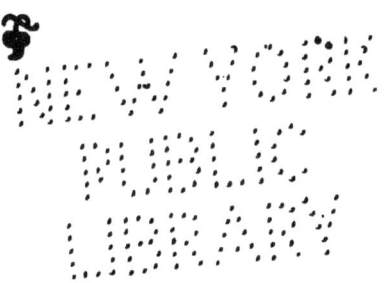

BOSTON:
PUBLISHED BY GEORGE B. REED,
LAW PUBLISHER.
1896.

Copyright, 1896,
BY SIDNEY PERLEY.

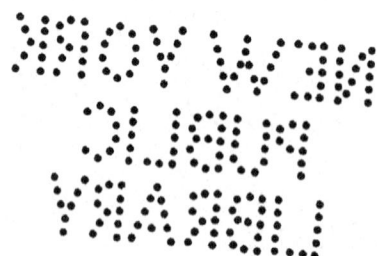

𝔘𝔫𝔦𝔳𝔢𝔯𝔰𝔦𝔱𝔶 𝔓𝔯𝔢𝔰𝔰:
JOHN WILSON AND SON, CAMBRIDGE, U.S.A.

PREFACE.

IN this volume it is endeavored to show the principles that underlie all law concerning dead human bodies. In modern times, because of the increase of population, for sanitary reasons, and on account of the large amount of money that is expended for funerals, for monuments, and for the care of burial places, the subject becomes increasingly important. The various legislatures have changed and extended the common law in some respects; but the great body of mortuary common law continues to be maintained in the United States.

SIDNEY PERLEY.

SALEM, MASS.,
    October 17, 1896.

NEW YORK
PUBLIC
LIBRARY

CONTENTS.

Chapter		Page
I.	Last Sickness	1
II.	Record of Deaths and Burials	9
III.	Inquests	11
IV.	Mutilation of Dead Bodies	20
V.	Property in Dead Bodies	23
VI.	Custody of Dead Bodies	26
VII.	Disposition of Dead Bodies	30
	The Right of Burial	30
	The Duty of Burial	36
	Manner of Disposition	39
VIII.	Undertakers	48
IX.	Funerals	51
X.	Funeral Expenses	59
XI.	Monuments, Gravestones, etc.	86
XII.	Permits to Transport, Bury, and Exhume Dead Bodies	100
XIII.	Transportation of Dead Bodies	103
XIV.	Exhumation of Dead Bodies	109
XV.	Cemeteries	114
	Tombs	114
	What constitutes a Cemetery	117
	Establishment of Cemeteries	119
	Kinds of Cemeteries	119

CONTENTS.

Chapter		Page
XVI.	Prohibition of Cemeteries	133
XVII.	Acquirement of Cemetery Lands	136
	By Prescription	136
	By Dedication	137
	By Conveyance	141
	By Right of Eminent Domain	142
	Reversion	147
XVIII.	Cemeteries as Nuisances	149
XIX.	Cemeteries as Charities	155
XX.	Rules and Regulations	159
XXI.	Taxation	162
XXII.	Sale, Mortgage, and Partition of Cemetery Property	169
	Sale of Cemetery Property	169
	Mortgage of Cemetery Property	170
	Partition of Cemetery Property	171
XXIII.	Care and Conduct of Cemeteries	172
XXIV.	Rights and Liabilities of Lot Owners	177
XXV.	Replevin	189
XXVI.	Larceny	191
XXVII.	Desecration of Cemeteries	192
XXVIII.	Opening Highways through Cemeteries	196
XXIX.	Abolition of Cemeteries	199
XXX.	Jurisdiction of Courts	208

Index 211

TABLE OF CASES CITED.

Accounting of James Frazier et al., ex'rs, 95.
    M. F. Reynolds, ex'r, 67.
Adams, adm'r, v. Butts, 83.
Adams' ex'rs v. Jones' adm'r, 8.
Allegheny County v. Watt, 17, 18.
Ambrose v. Kerrison, 74, 81, 82.
Andrews v. Cawthorne, 121.
Anonymous, 12.
Antrim et al., tr's, v. Malsbury et al., 124, 128.
Appeal of Ann M'Glinsey, adm'x, 67, 90.
Appeal Tax Court v. Baltimore Cemetery Co., 164.
    v. Zion Church of Baltimore, 164, 165.
Application of St. Bernard & St. Lawrence Cemetery Association, 124, 131, 145, 151.
Ashbury v. Sanders, 8.
Ashby v. Harris, 187.
Attorney General et al. v. Mayor, &c. of City of Newark, 199, 201.
Austin et al. v. Murray, 159, 160.

Bainbridge's Appeal, 94.
Barnes v. Hathorn, 131, 149–153.
Bartlett et al., ex'rs et tr's, petitioners, 155, 156.
Bates, adm'r, v. Bates, 155, 156.
Beatty et al. v. Trustees of German Lutheran Church of Georgetown, 117, 147.
Begein et al. v. City of Anderson, 149, 151, 161.
Bendall's distributees v. Bendall's adm'r, 89, 91.
Bennett et al. v. Culver, 130.

Bessemer Land & Improvement Co. v. Jenkins, 112, 204.
Birkholm v. Wardell et al., 68, 69.
Blaney v. State, 14, 16.
Bloomington Cemetery Association v. People, 162, 164, 165.
Board of Street Opening, &c. v. St. John's Cemetery, 196.
Bogert v. City of Indianapolis, 23, 33, 41, 159, 172.
Bonham v. Loeb, 111, 177.
Bourland v. Springdale Cemetery Association, 129, 130, 172, 185.
    v. Springdale Cemetery Association et al., 173.
Bourland et al. v. Springdale Cemetery Association, 185.
    v. Springdale Cemetery Association et al., 129, 172.
Bowditch v. Jordan, 8.
Boyce et al. v. Kalbaugh et al., 140, 210.
Bradshaw v. Beard, 76, 81.
Brendle et al. v. German Reformed Congregation et al., 142.
Brice v. Wilson, 71, 74, 75, 83.
Brick Presbyterian Church v. Mayor, &c. of City of New York, 151.
Brown v. Curé, &c. of Montreal, 180.
    v. Lutheran Church, 171.
Bryan v. Whistler, 122.
Buffalo City Cemetery v. City of Buffalo, 164, 167, 178.
Burke v. Wall et al., 184.
Burnett v. Noble, 93.
Butrick v. Tilton, 8.

Campbell v. City of Kansas, 139, 147, 148, 199–203.
    v. Purdy, 90.
Campfield, ex'r, v. Ely et al., 64.
Chapple v. Cooper, 81.
Christy v. Whitmore et al., 127.
City of Austin v. Austin City Cemetery Association, 159.
City of Baltimore v. Proprietors of Green Mount Cemetery, 163.
City of Greencastle v. Hazelett, 153.
City of Hoboken v. Inhabitants of North Bergen, 165.
City of New Castle v. Stone Church Graveyard, 164.
City of New Orleans v. Wardens of the Church of St. Louis, 149, 150.

City Council of Charleston v. Wentworth Street Baptist Church, 134.
Clark County v. Calloway, 12, 18.
    v. Kerstan, 18, 19.
    v. Lawrence, tr., 152, 153.
Coates v. Mayor, &c. of City of New York, 202.
Commissioners of Bartholomew County v. Jameson, 17, 19.
Commissioners of Dearborn County v. Bond, 17.
Commissioners of Dubois County v. Wertz, 19.
Commonwealth v. Cooley, 109, 113.
    v. Goodrich, 50, 159, 160.
    v. Harman, 17, 18.
    v. Thompson, 8.
    v. Viall, 126, 129, 138, 174, 175, 187, 194.
    v. Wellington, 126, 195, 199.
Concordia Cemetery Association v. Minnesota & Northwestern R. R. Co., 117, 118, 197.
Conger v. Treadway, 178.
Constantinides v. Walsh, ex'r, 37, 78, 81.
Cook et al. v. Walley & Rollins et al., 21, 101.
Cornwell v. Deck, 89.
County Commissioners of Pueblo v. Marshall et al., 17.
County of Allegheny v. Shaw et al., 17.
County of Lancaster v. Mishler, 12, 18.
County of Northampton v. Innes, 17, 18.
Craig et al. v. First Presbyterian Church of Pittsburgh, 200–202, 204, 206.
Crapo, ex'r, v. Armstrong, 86, 88, 91.
Crawford v. Elliott, 8.
Crisfield v. Perine, 17.
Crowell v. Londonderry, 133.
Cunningham v. Reardon, 37, 73, 76–78, 81.

Dalrymple v. Arnold, adm'r, 81.
Dampier v. St. Paul Trust Co., 71, 79.
Davidson v. Read et al., 137, 195.
Davie v. Briggs, 8.
Dawson v. Small, 155–157.
Day v. Beddingfield et al., 98, 120, 123, 193.

Dean and Chapter of Exeter's Case, 121.
Deansville Cemetery Association, 144, 146.
Detwiller v. Hartman, 155, 156.
Doe v. Pitcher et al., 155, 156.
Doe et al. v. Andrews et al., 8.
 v. Deakin et al., 8.
Dolan et al. v. Mayor, &c. of City of Baltimore, 147.
Domina Regina v. Clerk, 15.
Dominus Rex v. Bond, 13, 14.
 v. Stikeley, 14.
Donald v. McWhorter, 67, 71, 87.
Donnelly v. Boston Catholic Cemetery Association, 155, 186.
Du Bois Cemetery Co. v. Griffin et al., 198.
Dunn v. City of Austin, 149, 151, 152.
Durell v. Hayward, 37, 88.
 v. Walker et al., 33.
Dwenger et al. v. Geary et al., 124, 161, 179, 180.

Edwards v. Edwards, adm'x, 71.
Edwards et ux. v. Stonington Cemetery Association, 119.
Ellison v. Commissioners of Washington, 149, 150, 154.
Emans, ex'r, v. Hickman et al., 92.
Estate of Alfred Allen, 64, 68–70, 90.
 G. A. Erlacher, 71, 89.
 John S. Hill, 37, 75, 77, 78, 81.
 Emma J. Luchy, 93.
 Susan B. Miller, 74.
 Owen Rooney, 72, 89.
 Adna Wood, 66.
Evangelical Lutheran Cemetery Association v. Lange, assessor, 166.
Evergreen Cemetery Association v. City of New Haven, 143, 176, 197.
Evergreen Cemetery Association of New Haven v. Beecher et al, 143, 146.
Ex parte Anderson, 16.
 Blackmore, 121, 122.
 James M'Annully, 14.

TABLE OF CASES CITED.

Farneman et al. *v.* Mount Pleasant Cemetery Association, 142.
Fay *v.* Fay, 84.
Fay et al. *v.* Inhabitants of Milford, 127, 182.
Ferrin *v.* Myrick, adm'r, 36, 59, 80.
Fiske *v.* Attorney General, 155, 156.
Flintham's Appeal, 66.
Foley *v.* Phelps, 20, 26.
Foley, adm'r, *v.* Bushway, 87, 88.
Ford, &c. *v.* Ford's ex'r, 91, 92.
Foster *v.* Dodd et al., 23, 113, 208.
Foulks *v.* Rhea, 8.
Fowler *v.* Fowler, 155, 156.
France's Estate, 63, 74.
F. R. B. Cemetery Association *v.* Redd, 142, 144–146.
Freeman, ex'r, *v.* Coit et al., 6, 78, 81.
Fryar *v.* Johnson, 122.

Gilbert *v.* Buzzard et al., 41, 55, 121.
Gilmer's legatees *v.* Gilmer's ex'rs, 157.
Graves *v.* City of Bloomington, 100, 101.
Green *v.* Salmon, 78.
Gregory *v.* Hooker's adm'r, 59, 73, 74, 77, 78, 83, 84.
Griggs, adm'r, *v.* Veghte et al., 86, 91.
Griswold et al. *v.* Chandler, 64.
Gumbert's Appeal, 141, 148.
Guthrie *v.* Weaver, 23, 32, 34, 35, 112, 189.

Hackett *v.* Hackett, 33.
Hadsell et al. *v.* Hadsell et al., 23, 27, 33, 83.
Hagaman *v.* Dittmar, 138.
Hale *v.* Bonner et al., 104.
Hamilton *v.* City of New Albany, 187.
Hancock *v.* McAvoy, 187.
    v. Metz, 8.
    v. Podmore, ex'x, 71.
Hapgood *v.* Houghton, ex'r, 78, 83.
Hartson, ex'r, *v.* Elden et al., 155–157.
Hasler *v.* Hasler, 62, 63.

Hayes v. Hauke et al., 138.
Haynes' Case, 191.
Herbert v. Pue, 132.
Hewett v. Bronson, 60, 61.
Hicks et al. v. Danford et al., 137.
Hoare v. Osborne, 155, 156.
Hodge v. Blanton, 132.
Holmes et al. v. Johnson, 8.
Hook, &c. v. Joyce, 119, 136, 137.
Houston Cemetery Co. et al. v. Drew et al., 131, 174, 183.
Howard's Estate, 95.
Hoyt v. Newbold, 8.
Hullman et al. v. Honcamp et al., 139.
Humphrey et al. v. Trustees of M. E. Church, 184.
Hunter v. Bullock, 155, 156.
    v. Trustees of Sandy Hill, 137, 140.
Huse v. Brown, ex'r, 3.

Ingles' Estate, 94.
In re Birkett, 155, 156.
    Mutual Benefit Co., 8.
    Rector, &c. of St. George-in-the-East, 209.
    Wachter's Estate, 65.
    Williams, 155, 156.
    Wong Yung Quy, 110.

Jameson v. Commissioners of Bartholomew County, 12, 17-19.
Jamison v. Smith, 8.
Jenkins v. Tucker, 34, 37, 38, 70, 75, 81.
Jenkins et al. v. Inhabitants of Andover et al., 175.
Johnson v. Baker, 64.
Jones v. Ashburnham et ux., 23.

Kanavan's Case, 40, 41, 47, 55.
Keet v. Smith et al , 97.
Kemp v. Wickes, 32, 121.
Kincaid's Appeal, 109, 110, 179, 181-183, 207.
King v. Coleridge et al., 121, 208.
    v. Evett, 15.

King v. Soleguard et al., 12, 14.
Kingsbury v. Flowers, 149, 154.
Kittle v. Huntley, 72, 79.

Laird et al. v. Arnold, adm'r, 88.
    v. Arnold, adm'r, et al., 87.
Lake Erie & Western R. R. Co. v. James, 103.
Lakin v. Ames et al., 33, 116, 126.
Lancaster County v. Dern, 11, 12.
    v. Holyoke, 12, 15, 18.
Lang v. Commissioners of Perry County, 18.
Larson v. Chase, 20, 26, 27, 33.
Lautz v. Buckingham, 171.
Lawall et al. v. Keidler, ex'r, 82.
Lentz v. Pilert, 62, 77, 79.
Lerch, adm'r, v. Emmett et al., 87.
Lewis v. Walker's ex'rs, 188.
Lightbown v. M'Myn, 78, 81, 82.
Lima v. Lima Cemetery Association, 164, 168.
Lloyd v. Lloyd, 155, 156.
Loring v. Steinman, 8.
Louisville v. Nevins, &c., 162, 163.
Lucas v. Hessen et al., 78, 81, 83.
Lucy v. Walrond, adm'r, 73.
Lund v. Lund, 60, 90.

Marden v. City of Boston, 8.
Matter of Brick Presbyterian Church, 23, 116, 193, 194, 205, 206.
McCue, adm'r, v. Garvey, 31, 37, 55, 59, 63, 64, 73, 74, 76, 78, 79, 81.
McGough v. Lancaster Burial Board, 182.
McGuire, adm'r, v. Trustees of St. Patrick's Cathedral, 179–181.
Meagher v. Driscoll, 24, 110.
Mease v. Wagner, 79, 82.
Miller v. Morton et al., 72.
Mitchell et al. v. Thorne, 193–195.
Mitchelstown Inquisition, The, 15.
Monk v. Packard et al., 149, 150, 152, 153.
Montgomery v. Bevans, 7.

TABLE OF CASES CITED.

Moore's ex'r v. Moore et al., 155, 156.
Moreland et al. v. Richardson et al., 170, 183, 193.
Moulton, adm'r, v. Smith, adm'r, 6, 79, 81, 86.
Mowry v. City of Providence, 139, 140.
M. P. Church of Cincinnati v. Laws et al., 141.
Mt. Moriah Cemetery Association v. Commonwealth, 102, 161.
Mulroy v. Churchman et al., 165.
Musgrove v. Catholic Church of St. Louis, 149.

Neilson v. Brown et al., 26, 51.
Nevill v. Bridger, 122.
Newcombe v. Beloe et al., 75, 78.
N. Y. Bay Cemetery Co. v. Buckmaster, 178.
    v. Buckmaster et al., 130.
Nichols v. Eddy, 104.

Oak Hill Cemetery Association v. Pratt et al., assessors, 167.
Oakland Cemetery Co. v. Bancroft, 170, 171.
Olive Cemetery Co. v. City of Philadelphia, 163.
Ommaney v. Stilwell, 7.
Owens v. Bloomer, adm'x, et al., 86, 90.

Pacie v. Archbishop of Canterbury, 66.
Page v. Symonds et al., 181, 182, 184.
Palmes et al. v. Stephens, 7, 71.
Parker, adm'r, v. Lewis, adm'r, 59, 77.
Partridge et al. v. First Independent Church of Baltimore, 179, 182, 183, 204, 206.
Patterson, ex'x, v. Patterson, 59, 74.
People v. Devine, 14.
    v. Fitzgerald, 13.
    v. Graceland Cemetery Co., 166.
    v. Graves, 113.
Percival, adm'r, v. McVoy, 3, 4, 6.
Perkins v. City of Lawrence, 174, 188.
Peters v. Peters et al., 35, 111.
Philadelphia v. Westminster Cemetery Co., 133.
Phillips v. Phillips, 84.

Pierce v. Spafford, 128, 139, 172, 186.
Pierce et ux. v. Proprietors of Swan Point Cemetery et al., 23–25, 31, 32, 35, 37, 39, 78, 102, 109, 112, 115, 121, 122, 131, 193, 208.
Polly Fairman's Appeal, 69, 87, 89–91, 97, 99.
Porter's Estate, 86, 95.
Price et al. v. M. E. Church et al., 124, 183, 205.
Proprietors of Cemetery of Mount Auburn v. Mayor, &c. of Cambridge et al., 162, 168.
Proprietors of Rural Cemetery v. County Commissioners of Worcester, 166, 168.
Protestant Foster Home v. Mayor, &c. of City of Newark, 163.
Pyle et al., ex'rs, v. Pyle et al., 16.

Queen v. Clerk, 12, 13, 15.
    v. Fox et al., 23, 28.
    v. Herford, 14.
    v. Price, 19, 31, 45, 46.
    v. Shepherd, 16.
    v. Stephenson et al., 19.
    v. Stewart et al., 41, 32, 38, 57, 83.
    v. Twiss, 209.
    v. Twiss, judge, 196.

Rappelyea v. Russell, 59, 61, 74, 77–79.
Rayner v. Nugent et al., adm'rs, 179, 181, 183.
Redwood Cemetery Association v. Bandy et al., 137, 141.
Reed et al. v. Stouffer et al., 141, 202.
Reese Estate, 3.
Regina v. Sharpe, 23, 27, 34, 109.
    v. Taylor, 16.
    v. Vann, 33, 38.
    v. White et al., 19.
Renihan et al. v. Wright et al., 28, 37, 49.
Rex v. Long, 15.
    v. Nicholas et al., 15.
Richards v. Northwest Protestant Dutch Church, 204, 205.
Rickard v. Robson, 155, 156.
Ritchey v. City of Canton, 159.

Rogers v. Price, 74, 76, 78, 83.
Root et al. v. Odd Fellows Cemetery Co., 119.
Rosehill Cemetery Co. v. Hopkinson, ex'x, 161, 184.
Ruggles' Report, 32, 36, 113.
Rust v. Baker, 8.
Ryan v. Tudor et al., 8.

Sabin et al., ex'rs, v. Harkness, 193, 194.
Salvo & Wade v. Schmidt, 59.
Samuel v. Estate of John Thomas, 79.
Schroder v. Wanzor, 169.
Sears v. Giddey, 80.
Secor's Case, 100.
Sensenderfer v. Pacific Mutual Life Insurance Co., 8.
Seymour v. Page, 174, 183, 187, 188.
Sharp v. Lush, 59.
Sheldon v. Ferris et al., 8.
Shown v. Mackin, 8.
Silverwood v. Latrobe et al., 187.
Smiley et al. v. Bartlett et al., 27, 32, 34, 184.
Smith v. Thompson, 186.
Smyley, adm'r, v. Reese et al., 80.
Sohier et al. v. Trinity Church et al., 115, 203.
Spears v. Burton, 8.
Spooner v. Brewster, 98, 99, 123, 193, 195.
Stag v. Punter, 72.
Staple's Appeal, 80, 81.
State v. Doepke, 191.
    v. Evans, 15.
    v. Wilson, 137, 140.
    v. Wilson, &c., 164.
State, &c. v. City of St. Paul, 163, 164.
Stevens v. Town of Norfolk, 199.
Stewart's Appeal, 69.
St. Francis County v. Cummings, 17–19.
St. John's Cemetery, 200, 203.
Stockbridge, petitioner, 8.
Sullivan v. Horner, adm'r, 31, 36, 37, 59, 62, 63, 71, 74, 82.
Sweeney v. Muldoon, adm'r, 32, 86, 88.

Tate v. State, 110.
Thomas v. Thomas, 8.
Tilly v. Tilly, 8.
Town of Lake View v. Letz et al., 150, 151.
    v. Rose Hill Cemetery Co., 128, 134, 149-151, 173.
Trueman v. Tilden, 80.
Trustees of First Evangelical Church et al. v. Walsh et al., 198.
Tugwell v. Heyman et al., ex'rs, 59, 70, 74.
Tuttle, adm'r, v. Robinson, 99.
Tyler v. Tyler, 158.

United States v. Eggleston et al., 2.
University of North Carolina v. Harrison et al., 8.
Upjohn v. Board of Health et al., 135, 210.

Valentine v. Valentine, 68.
Van Emon et al. v. Superior Court, 86.
Van Hoevenbergh v. Habrouck, coroner, 18.
Van Orden v. Krouse et al., 84.
Vaughn v. Thomas, 155.
Village of Hyde Park v. Oakwoods Cemetery Association, 197.

Walker et al., com'rs, v. Sheftall, 77, 83.
Wall Street M. E. Church v. Johnson et al., 124.
Ward & Co. v. Jones, adm'r, 59, 77.
Weld v. Walker et al., 23, 34, 37, 109, 111, 210.
Went v. M. P. Church of Williamsburgh et al., 151, 177, 184, 201-203.
Wentworth v. Wentworth, 8.
White Lick Quarterly Meeting, &c. v. White Lick Quarterly Meeting, &c., 180.
Willeter v. Dobie, 78, 81, 82.
Williams v. Stonestreet, et ux., 6.
    v. Williams, 23, 28, 29, 32, 37, 45.
Willis v. Jones et al., assignees, 37, 80.
Willis' adm'r, v. Heirs of Willis, 64.
Wilson et al. v. Staats, ex'r, 82.
Windt et al. v. German Reformed Church, 204, 205.

Winship v. Conner, 8.
Wolford v. Crystal Lake Cemetery Association, 170.
Wonson v. Sayward, 191.
Wood et al. v. Macon and Brunswick R. R. Co. et al., 172, 173, 197.
  v. Vandenburgh et al., 91.
Woods v. Woods' adm'r, 8.
Wright v. Wallasey Local Board, 133.
Wynkoop v. Wynkoop, 27, 31–33, 36–38, 112.

Young v. College of Physicians and Surgeons et al., 17, 21.
  v. Heffner, 8.

Zirngibl v. Calument, &c. Canal & Dock Co., 136.

MORTUARY LAW.

CHAPTER I.

LAST SICKNESS.

The subject of mortuary law naturally begins with a person's last sickness. Until the time he is overtaken by that physical condition which terminates his life, the common rules of law, as of contract relations, etc., apply. But when that time arrives new rules come into application and enforcement. This new phase of a man's relations arises from the necessity of his condition. The law will allow no one to suffer for want of necessary care and medical treatment while in his extremity.

At common law there is little occasion for defining and applying the term. Perhaps the most common instance is that where a parent conveys property to his child on condition of the child's support of such parent during the latter's lifetime, together with the expenses of his last sickness. Another instance is in the case of a will, in which the testator devises certain estate, charging upon it the expenses of his last sickness, etc.

But under the statutes the matter of the last sickness

becomes much more important, especially in the settlement of insolvent estates, as in most of the States in the Union such expenses are preferred over ordinary and over many extraordinary debts, and in some States actions can be brought for them before suits for the enforcement of ordinary claims. In Alabama,[1] for instance, such expenses occupy the third place in priority of claims, as follows: 1. The funeral expenses; 2. Charges of administration; 3. Expenses of last sickness; 4. Taxes; 5. Employees' services; 6. Other debts. They have priority also over claims due to the United States.[2]

Duration of Last Sickness. — The first question that arises in relation to the subject of last sickness is in reference to the duration of what can be legally called a man's last sickness. All people that have died have not had such a sickness. Those who have been exempt, either died by their own hand, or have had their lives taken by accident, legal process, or war. In all these exceptional cases there is no medical attendance and no nursing. It is not intended that in this enumeration any one should be included who lingers awhile after an attempt upon his life, nor any other who does not immediately die after the receipt of a mortal wound. Generally, there is a period in which a person is afflicted with some disease which continues to affect him physically until it causes his death. This must be the primary cause of his decease. If it is a congenital disease, or organic defection simply, the last sickness must be accounted as beginning with that change in his condition for the

---

[1] Alabama Code, 1886, § 2079.
[2] *United States* v. *Eggleston et al.*, 4 Sawyer (U. S.) 199 (1877).

worse which is generally plainly perceptible; for this rule does not rest upon the assumption that every person is physically perfect and healthful. A person may have an organic disease which must, if nothing else that is fatal intervenes, eventually produce death, and may at times be so enfeebled and so sick therewith as to forbid hope of recovery, and yet he may again become comparatively well. The last sickness arising from such a disease or organic condition is not such a sickness, unless in that particular instance death results. Such cases are those of cancer, which are apparently cured by extraction or otherwise, and again and again break out, finally causing death. In consumption, the period of last sickness begins at the time when a person is decidedly enfeebled and needs special treatment, and after which he never really returns to his normal condition, but the disease gains control over the system, though the subject may at times seem to recover some new strength. There is no definite rule, of course, that can be laid down to govern as to the beginning of the last sickness in every case. It must vary with the many different diseases and causes of death; and it should be left to the jury to determine in each particular case.[1] The policy of the law is to be liberal in this respect, that every person may receive all the attention and care and skill which his condition demands, the financial part of the question being secondary.[2]

The last sickness in its termination is more certain. Death ends it abruptly.

[1] *Huse* v. *Brown, ex'r*, 8 Maine 167 (1831); *Reese Estate*, 2 Pearson (Pa.) 482.

[2] *Percival, adm'r*, v. *McVoy*, Dudley (S. C.) 337 (1838).

Character of Service and Expenses. — What are the expenses of the last sickness of a person? It is clear that medical attendance, nursing,[1] medicine, and some articles peculiarly proper and necessary to be used in the kind of sickness in each particular case are necessary and come within such service and expenses. It is doubtful if food, clothing, bed linen, etc., can be included. The expense of tolling a church bell upon the decease of a person, or of sounding the passing bell[2] while the decedent is quitting the scenes of this life, if such practice is in vogue in any place now, is certainly not within the legitimate bounds of the expenses of the last sickness.

[1] *Percival, adm'r*, v. *McVoy*, Dudley (S. C.) 337 (1838).

[2] The passing bell, or soul bell, began to be rung as soon as it was apparent that death would ensue within a few minutes. It was an ancient custom, being common in the days of the monastery system, and Bede wrote of it. It was thought to ward off evil spirits from the departing soul. The more modern custom of tolling the bell immediately after the decease of a person is the later method of ringing the passing bell. Grose says: "The passing bell was anciently rung for two purposes: one to bespeak the prayers of all good Christians for a soul just departing; the other to drive away the evil spirits who stood at the bed's foot and about the house, ready to seize their prey, or at least to molest and terrify the soul in its passage; but, by the ringing of the bell (for Durandus informs us that evil spirits are much afraid of bells), they were kept aloof; and the soul like a hunted hare, gained the start, or had what is by sportsmen called law. Hence, perhaps, exclusive of the additional labour, was occasioned the high price demanded for tolling the greatest bell of the church, for, that being louder, the evil spirits must go farther off to be clear of its sound, by which the poor soul got so much the start of them; besides, being heard farther off, it would likewise procure the dying man a greater number of prayers."

Who is Responsible for the Expenses? — On general principles, a person, and also his estate, is liable only for such debts as he has contracted. He must have had the natural and legal ability to contract, and be shown to have contracted, either directly or through an agent. He and his estate are liable for every contract he legally makes for medical attendance, nursing, etc. But when a man is unable, through physical or mental disability, to make these contracts in his last sickness, the extraordinary rules of the law of necessity arise and make such contracts as he would be presumed to make for himself if he was able to do so. This policy of the law arises from the necessity of the situation to prevent suffering and to insure to every person comfort and humane treatment. If this was not the law it would be difficult for people generally to receive any medical treatment or nursing beyond that prompted by feelings of love or humanity, often involving even in such cases great sacrifices on the part of those who could not afford to give time and money to the relief of the sick. These extraordinary rules cast the payment for such services and expenses upon the subject's estate, and this insures comfort and good treatment and care in a man's extremity. In cases of this kind the person who engages the physician or the nurse or procures the medicines and other necessary articles is presumed to be the agent of the sick one.

There is one exception to the rule that a person's estate must pay the expense of his or her last sickness. When some one other than the decedent has the duty of supporting him or her, that person must pay the cost. In the case of husband and wife, the husband is personally chargeable with the expenses of her last sickness, and her estate is not responsible therefor, either primarily or secondarily.[1]

There is also a duty upon the members of each family to care for one another without pay. In the case of *Williams* v. *Stonestreet et ux.*,[2] a son-in-law of the deceased was not allowed to recover for his services in nursing him, there being no contract, either express or implied, that the services should be paid for.

Amount Allowed for Expenses. — The situation of the patient has a great deal to do with the amount of service to be rendered. If he is in a home of his own, which has the conveniences of housekeeping, etc., much less expense of procuring articles is necessary, than if he was sick in a place where things essential to his comfort or treatment would have to be purchased for his special use. The nature of the sickness is another important factor in the amount of care and treatment that is reasonably necessary and proper. A man that can move about can help himself in many ways, but one who is confined to his bed must be waited on. One who is delirious requires extreme care and attention. Fine distinctions and niceties of arithmetic are out of place in the application of this law of necessity; it should be liberally applied,[3] for a man's estate cannot be better employed than in ministering to his comfort during his last earthly hours, and humanity demands that no one shall suffer.

[1] *Freeman, ex'r,* v. *Coit et al.*, 27 Hun (N. Y.) 447 (1882); *Moulton, adm'r,* v. *Smith, adm'r*, 16 R. I. 126 (1888).

[2] *Williams* v. *Stonestreet et ux.*, 3 Rand. (Va.) 559 (1825).

[3] *Percival, adm'r,* v. *McVoy*, Dudley (S. C.) 337 (1838).

Neither in England nor the United States can the proper amount to be allowed for expenses of this kind be determined by the rank of the decedent.[1]

If the contract price for the labor and articles was agreed upon by the decedent, who was legally able to contract, and whose estate is to pay the bills, that price must be paid if the estate is solvent. In all other cases, the court can only allow the market price of the labor and articles, which is to be found by a jury in the ordinary manner. The fair market price is the rule.

Presumption of Death. — Although the subject of mortuary law deals only with actual death and dead bodies, the thought of the law of presumption of death naturally arises in connection therewith. In the early common law there was no such presumption. If a man was proven to have been alive, he was presumed to continue to live,[2] unless an unnatural age would thus be shown; but even then there was no legal presumption.

A statute was early enacted in England creating the presumption of death where parties had been out of the State or country, and unheard of by their family and acquaintances in the place of their last abode for seven years. In America this statute has the effect of common law, and some of the States have placed it among their statutes. The presumption arises when a person leaves his fixed home for temporary purposes, and is not again heard from for seven years by those who would naturally hear from

[1] *Palmes et al.* v. *Stephens*, R. M. Charlton (Ga.) 56 (1821).
[2] *Ommaney* v. *Stillwell*, 23 Beav. (Eng.) 328 (1856); *Montgomery* v. *Bevans*, 1 Sawyer (U. S.) 660 (1871).

him if he was alive.[1] But it does not arise in the case of a man who leaves the country as an absconder.[2]

This presumption does not admit that a person died before the expiration of the seven years, unless there is evidence that he was at some particular date previous thereto under a specific peril.[3]

Courts should be slow to grant letters of administration, and parties to receive them, when the decease of the subject of them is not clearly shown, as death only gives the court jurisdiction, as a general rule.[4]

[1] *Doe et al.* v. *Deakin et al.*, 4 Barn. & Ald. (Eng.) 433 (1821); *Rust* v. *Baker*, 8 Sim. (Eng.) 443 (1837); *Doe et al.* v. *Andrews et al.*, 15 Ad. & El., N. S., (Eng.) 760 (1850); *Davie* v. *Briggs*, 7 Otto (U. S.) 628 (1878); *Ashbury* v. *Sanders*, 8 Cal. 62 (1857); *Crawford* v. *Elliott*, 1 Houst. (Del.) 465 (1857); *Adams' ex'rs* v. *Jones' adm'r*, 39 Ga. 508 (1869); *Ryan* v. *Tudor et al.*, 31 Kansas 366 (1884); *Foulks* v. *Rhea*, 7 Bush (Ky.) 568 (1870); *Jamison* v. *Smith*, 35 La. Ann. 609 (1883); *Wentworth* v. *Wentworth*, 71 Me. 72 (1880); *Tilly* v. *Tilly*, 2 Bland. Ch. (Md.) 436 (1831); *Loring* v. *Steineman*, 1 Met. (Mass.) 204 (1840); *Commonwealth* v. *Thompson*, 11 Allen (Mass.) 23 (1865); *Bowditch* v. *Jordan*, 131 Mass. 321 (1881); *Stockbridge, petitioner*, 145 Mass. 517 (1888); *Marden* v. *City of Boston*, 155 Mass. 359 (1892); *Butrick* v. *Tilton*, 155 Mass. 462 (1892); *Spears* v. *Burton*, 31 Miss. 547 (1856); *Thomas* v. *Thomas*, 16 Neb. 553 (1884); *Winship* v. *Conner*, 42 N. H. 341 (1861); *Hoyt* v. *Newbold*, 45 N. J. L. 219 (1883); *Sheldon* v. *Ferris et al.*, 45 Barb. (N. Y.) 124 (1865); *University of North Carolina* v. *Harrison et al.*, 90 N. C. 385 (1884); *Young* v. *Heffner*, 36 Ohio St. 232 (1880); *Holmes et al.* v. *Johnson*, 42 Pa. St. 159 (1862); *Woods* v. *Woods' adm'r*, 2 Bay (S. C.) 476 (1802); *Shown* v. *Mackin*, 9 Lea (Tenn.) 601 (1882); *Hancock* v. *Metz*, 7 Texas 178 (1851).

[2] *Sensenderfer* v. *Pacific Mutual Life Insurance Co.*, 19 Fed. Rep. (Mo.) 68 (1882).

[3] *Davie* v. *Briggs*, 7 Otto (U. S.) 628 (1878); *In re Mutual Benefit Co.*, 34 Atl. Rep. (Pa.) 283 (1896).

[4] *Shown* v. *Mackin*, 9 Lea (Tenn.) 601 (1882).

CHAPTER II.

RECORD OF DEATHS AND BURIALS.

By the common law, no record of deaths or burials is required to be kept. Most of the States now provide by statute for the registration of the decease of persons who die within their borders, and of others who are residents, but who have died without their limits, and of the burial of those who have been interred in the town, under a penalty for its non-observance. Under these laws the registration is by towns and cities, and the records are made up of all necessary facts for the identification of the deceased. Perhaps the most complete system of registration exists in Massachusetts. By its aid, genealogies of families are traced and made certain by the large amount of data that is recorded, and the identification of each decedent is made certain. Physicians are required in many States to make return to the proper officer, in their respective localities, of the decease of persons whom they treated at the time of their death, and this return generally has to be as full and complete as the required record. If there was no physician in attendance upon the deceased, another's statement is sufficient. The enforcement of these statutes is made more compulsory by the fact that permits to bury issue from the registrar of deaths and only upon such return of death being filed either by the physician or undertaker.

The registration of burials is said to have been introduced into England in 1522 by Thomas Cromwell, who was then vicar general.

CHAPTER III.

INQUESTS.

AN inquest is an inquiry into the cause and manner of death of persons in certain cases. The purpose is twofold: to discover, first, the cause and manner of death, and, second, the person by whom it was caused, if the inquest shows that it was criminally produced.

In what Cases Inquests are held. — In a broad sense, inquests are held upon persons who died of a violent or an unnatural death, or where there is suspicion of foul play in the cause of death.[1] It is not necessary, at common law, that an inquest be held in the case of a person who died with fever, apoplexy, or other disease, and neither does any statute probably require this. Neither is it proper to inquire into cases of sudden deaths, unless there is reasonable ground to believe that they are the result of violence or unnatural means. The discretion of a sound mind and good judgment must be the measure of authority under which the coroner decides upon the necessity of the exercise of his office, the presumption being that he has acted in good faith and with sufficient

---

[1] *Lancaster County* v. *Dern,* 2 Grant's Cases (Pa.) 262 (1852).

cause.[1] This presumption of good faith is only *prima facie*, however.[2]

When death results from any violence done to one person by another, although the life of the person injured is not by that means immediately terminated, the coroner must hold an inquest.[3]

Statutes now quite generally govern inquests, and designate the classes of cases in which investigation is to be made.

Information of Death. — Under the old English law, an indictment would lie against a man who buried the body of a person who came to a violent death without notifying the proper authorities of the circumstances of the decease or finding of the body.[4] It was also a misdemeanor to allow a body to lie until putrefaction had set in before such notification.

Time of holding Inquest. — The inquest should be held immediately after the body is found, or the person dies.[5]

If the body has been buried before the inquest is held, the coroner must have it exhumed, and this he may lawfully do within a reasonable time.

---

[1] *Clark County* v. *Calloway*, 52 Ark. 361 (1889); *Lancaster County* v. *Holyoke*, 37 Neb. 328 (1893); *County of Lancaster* v. *Mishler*, 100 Pa. St. 624 (1882).

[2] *Jameson* v. *Board of Commissioners of Bartholomew County*, 64 Ind. 524 (1878); *County of Lancaster* v. *Mishler*, 100 Pa. St. 624 (1882).

[3] *Lancaster County* v. *Dern*, 2 Grant's Cases (Pa.) 262 (1852).

[4] *Anonymous*, 7 Mod. (Eng.), Case 15; *Queen* v. *Clerk*, Holt (Eng.) 167 (1702).

[5] *King* v. *Soleguard et al.*, Andrews (Eng.) 231 (1738).

Seven months is too long for it to lie buried,[1] unless probably it is a case in which there is suspicion of poisoning. But the coroner cannot exhume a body under any circumstances unless he complies with all the requirements of the law in regard thereto, as the summoning of a jury, etc.[2]

Place of holding Inquest. — The inquest must be held at the place where the decease of the person occurred, or the body is found.

By Whom the Inquest is held. — The ancient, as well as modern, title of the officer who is empowered to hold inquests is *coroner*, though in some States he is a statutory official and given the name of medical examiner. Judges of inferior courts of law are sometimes given jurisdiction in such cases. A coroner, so called from *coronator*, the officer with whom the King was more immediately concerned, was a common law official of broad powers, the chief coroner in the kingdom being the lord chief justice of the King's Bench, who had general jurisdiction throughout the realm. In England, and generally in America, they are county officers, several being appointed for and in each of such districts.

The choice of a coroner, etc., is provided for by statute or constitution in the American States, and in England he is elected by the freeholders in the county court. In early times, he must have been a

---

[1] *Queen* v. *Clerk,* Holt (Eng.) 167 (1702); *Dominus Rex* v. *Bond,* 1 Strange (Eng.) 22 (1716).

[2] *People* v. *Fitzgerald,* 43 Hun (N. Y.) 35 (1887). On appeal, in the same case, the court of appeals questioned the correctness of the decision of the supreme court. *People* v. *Fitzgerald,* 105 N. Y. 148 (1887).

knight, but now a person having landed property sufficient to enable him to receive the grant of knighthood can be chosen to the office of coroner without being knighted. Such is the principal qualification of a coroner in England, where he is a more important officer than in America, being chosen for life, though liable to be removed at any time for cause.

The Hearing. — The first requisite of an inquest is the presence of the body of the deceased. If the body has not been found, there cannot be a coroner's inquest;[1] and the presence of the head of the body alone is not sufficient.[2]

The inquest must be made by a jury of at least twelve men, summoned by the coroner from the vicinage of the place of death.[3] The coroner administers the oath to them, and presides over them during the hearing, constituting a coroner's court, which is judicial in its character,[4] and of such a nature that it can legally sit on Sunday.[5] After the jury are duly charged by the coroner as to their duties, they proceed to take a "view" of the body, which should be as when found so far as possible,[6] and hear evidence. The "view" is something more

[1] *Queen* v. *Herford*, 3 El. & El. (Eng.) 115 (1860).

[2] *Dominus Rex* v. *Bond*, 1 Strange (Eng.) 22 (1716).

[3] A juror, having been duly summoned, is liable to a fine for failing to attend the inquest. *Ex parte James M'Annully*, T. U. P. Charlton (Ga.) 310 (1810). A coroner cannot take a juryman off the panel after he has been sworn. *Dominus Rex* v. *Stikely*, Holt (Eng.) 167 (1701).

[4] *People* v. *Devine*, 44 Cal. 452 (1872).

[5] *Blaney* v. *State*, 74 Md. 153 (1891).

[6] *King* v. *Soleguard et al.*, Andrews (Eng.) 231 (1738).

than to take a look at the body; they must investigate and inspect it carefully and thoroughly.[1] They must seek to discover how the person came to his death, in all its particulars, when and where it occurred, who was present, by whom it was caused, if by a person, and the name and residence of the deceased; and to examine and describe all wounds, if any, their length, breadth, and depth, the kind of weapons that caused them, in what manner they caused them, on what part of the body the wounds were found, and whether or not the deceased died of the wounds.[2]

The coroner must receive the verdict of the jury in open court; the finding will be quashed if he takes it in their room.[3]

The jurors must sign their return,[4] and the coro-

---

[1] *Lancaster County* v. *Holyoke*, 37 Neb. 328 (1893).

[2] *Domina Regina* v. *Clerk*, 1 Salkeld (Eng.) 377 (1702); *Queen* v. *Clerk*, 7 Mod. (Eng.) 16 (1702).

[3] *The Mitchelstown Inquisition*, L. R. 22 Irish 279 (1888).

[4] The jurors may sign by their mark, if the coroner certifies that it was signed by them. *State* v. *Evans*, 27 La. Ann. 297 (1875). If several of the jurors have the same Christian and surname, they need not be distinguished by their abode or occupation. *Rex* v. *Nicholas et al.*, 7 C. & P. (Eng.) 538 (1836). If the jurors' names are written in full in the caption of the inquisition, their Christian names may be abbreviated in their signatures. *Rex* v. *Long*, 6 C. & P. (Eng.) 179 (1833). In the case of the *King* v. *Evett*, 6 B. & C. (Eng.) 247 (1827), an inquest was quashed because it omitted to state when the death occurred, or when the body was found, and the Christian names of the jurors were signed by their initials only, their names not being set out in the body of the inquisition.

The concluding averment, "And so the jurors do say," need not show either time or place. *Rex* v. *Nicholas et al.*, 7 C. & P. (Eng.) 538 (1836).

ner must certify to the whole of the inquest under his seal, together with the evidence thereon, to the next court held for the trial of murder cases.[1] If the jury finds that a person is probably criminally guilty of the death of the deceased, it is the duty of the coroner to commit such suspected party to jail for trial; and if forfeiture of his estate follows such a crime, the coroner must report concerning the character and extent of his property. The report of the coroner takes the place of an indictment, and the suspected person is not entitled to be taken before a magistrate for preliminary examination.[2] Such is the rule and practice in England and in one or two States in the American Union, but in the Constitution of the United States it is made imperative that a presentment or indictment of a grand jury be found.[3]

If the inquest shows the case to be criminal, and the party who is probably guilty is arrested, the coroner must bind over the witnesses who are to testify for the government to appear at the trial of the prisoner.[4]

Immediately after the inquest the body must be interred by the coroner or others.

Autopsy. — If the jury find that it is necessary to

[1] The certificate can be amended in matters of form. *Queen* v. *Shepherd*, 11 Mod. (Eng.) 271 (1710). The verdict is admissible as evidence in civil cases to show that the deceased committed suicide. *Pyle et al., ex'rs,* v. *Pyle et al.*, 158 Ill. 289 (1895).

[2] *Ex parte Anderson*, 55 Ark. 527 (1892). See *Blaney* v. *State*, 74 Md. 153 (1891).

[3] United States Constitution, Fifth Amendment.

[4] *Regina* v. *Taylor et al.*, 9 C. & P. (Eng.) 672 (1840).

the proper understanding of the condition of a dead body that a *post mortem* examination be made, the coroner is authorized to employ a physician or surgeon to make it,[1] and he has the choice of the physician or surgeon.[2] A physician engaged by a coroner for an autopsy or examination is not bound to know that the jury deem a *post mortem* examination necessary; he has a right to rely upon the official act of the coroner.[3] The coroner can permit whom he pleases to be present at such an examination; and a person under accusation cannot claim the right to be there.[4]

If the services of a chemist are needed to make an analysis of the stomach of a dead person, in cases where poisoning is suspected, the coroner has the authority to engage one, and may choose one who resides within or without the county, as he pleases.[5]

Expenses. — It is within the province of the county court to determine whether the case is one for the

[1] *St. Francis County* v. *Cummings*, 55 Ark. 419 (1892); *County Commissioners of Pueblo* v. *Marshall et al.*, 11 Col. 84 (1887); *Jameson* v. *Commissioners of Bartholomew County*, 64 Ind. 524 (1878); *Young* v. *College of Physicians and Surgeons et al.*, 81 Md. 358 (1895); *Allegheny County* v. *Watt*, 3 Pa. St. 462 (1846); *Commonwealth* v. *Harman*, 4 Pa. St. 269 (1846); *County of Northampton* v. *Innes*, 26 Pa. St. 156 (1856).

[2] *Commissioners of Dearborn County* v. *Bond*, 88 Ind. 102 (1882); *County of Allegheny* v. *Shaw et al.*, 34 Pa. St. 301 (1859).

[3] *County Commissioners of Pueblo* v. *Marshall et al.*, 11 Col. 84 (1887).

[4] *Crisfield* v. *Perine*, 15 Hun (N. Y.) 200 (1878); affirmed by the court of appeals, *Crisfield* v. *Perine*, 81 N. Y. 622 (1880).

[5] *Commissioners of Bartholomew County* v. *Jameson*, 86 Ind. 154 (1882).

expense of which the county is liable.[1] In all cases where the coroner has acted in good faith and with ordinary judgment he should be allowed his fees.[2] But he is not entitled to compensation unless he has summoned a jury, and proceeded as the law directs; as otherwise he has acquired no jurisdiction, and therefore no right to act in the case.[3] A reasonable remuneration for the services of the physician performing a *post mortem* examination must be paid.[4] If there is no special agreement between the physician and the coroner as to who shall pay the former for his professional services, the coroner alone can be sued. The physician cannot bring an action against the county therefor. The coroner must put the bill into his account against the county.[5] A physician who is employed to treat the poor of an asylum when sick is entitled to a reasonable fee for making an autopsy on the body of one of the paupers who came to his death by a casualty, when so requested by the coroner.[6] A physician who has performed such an autopsy is not entitled to extra

---

[1] *Clark County* v. *Calloway*, 52 Ark. 361 (1889).

[2] *County of Lancaster* v. *Mishler*, 100 Pa St. 624 (1882).

[3] *Lancaster County* v. *Holyoke*, 37 Neb. 328 (1893).

[4] *St. Francis County* v. *Cummings*, 55 Ark. 419 (1892); *Clark County* v. *Kerstan*, 60 Ark. 508 (1895); *Jameson* v. *Commissioners of Bartholomew County*, 64 Ind. 524 (1878); *Allegheny County* v. *Watt*, 3 Pa. St. 462 (1846); *Commonwealth* v. *Harman*, 4 Pa. St. 269 (1846); *County of Northampton* v. *Innes*, 26 Pa. St. 156 (1856).

[5] *Van Hoevenbergh* v. *Habrouck, coroner*, 45 Barb. (N. Y.) 197 (1865).

[6] *Lang* v. *Commissioners of Perry County*, 121 Ind. 133 (1889).

compensation as an expert witness beyond the regular witness fee.[1] Chemists performing analyses at the request of coroners, for the purposes of inquests, are also entitled to reasonable compensation for such services.[2]

Counties are generally responsible for the expenses of inquests.[3] By statute, in some of the American States, valuables on the bodies of persons who are found dead may be appropriated to the payment of the expense of the inquest held on such bodies; as for instance, in Indiana.

Interfering with Inquests. — It is a misdemeanor to burn or otherwise dispose of a dead body, with intent thereby to prevent the holding of an inquest, in a proper case, as it is an act obstructing the coroner in his duties.[4]

Second Inquests. — A second inquest cannot be legally held unless the first is quashed.[5]

---

[1] *Clark County* v. *Kerstan*, 60 Ark. 508 (1895).

[2] *Commissioners of Bartholomew County* v. *Jameson*, 86 Ind. 154 (1882).

[3] *St. Francis County* v. *Cummings*, 55 Ark. 419 (1892); *Clark County* v. *Kerstan*, 60 Ark. 508 (1895); *Jameson* v. *Commissioners of Bartholomew County*, 64 Ind. 524 (1878); *Commissioners of Dubois County* v. *Wertz*, 112 Ind. 268 (1887).

[4] *Queen* v. *Price*, L. R. 12 Q. B. Div. (Eng.) 247 (1884); *Queen* v. *Stephenson et al.*, L. R. 13 Q. B. Div. (Eng.) 331 (1884).

[5] *Regina* v. *White et al.*, 3 El. & El. (Eng.) 137 (1860).

CHAPTER IV.

MUTILATION OF DEAD BODIES.

It is the privilege and duty of certain relatives of deceased persons, as will be seen in Chapter VII., to preserve the remains from indecent and improper treatment, as well as to bury them. The law will protect this right and duty. Statutes, in many of the American States, fix the criminal liability of those who are guilty of its violation. For an unlawful mutilation of the remains,[1] a civil action will lie; and although no actual pecuniary loss has been suffered, substantial damages may be awarded for the injury to the feelings and mental sufferings naturally resulting directly and proximately from the wrongful act.[2]

When the law demands that mutilation of a dead body shall take place, the physician who commits the act is not responsible. As, for instance, where a physician makes a *post mortem* examination of a dead body, in the usual manner, at the request of a coroner acting officially, such physician is not liable in an action for damages to the family of the

---

[1] *Foley* v. *Phelps*, 37 N. Y. S. Rep. 471 (1896). This suit was brought by the widow of the deceased.

[2] *Larson* v. *Chase*, 47 Minn. 307 (1891).

deceased for the mutilation of the body done without their consent.[1] Also, where the ordinances of a city require a physician's certificate of the cause of death before burial of the body, and a *post mortem* examination is necessary to such certificate, an action for damages for mutilating the body will not lie in favor of the heirs of the deceased against the physician who makes the examination, nor the undertaker who requested it to be made, the autopsy being performed in a decent and scientific manner, due regard being had to the sex of the deceased, without undue exposure, and with respect to the feelings of the relatives who did not consent.[2]

The common form of mutilation of the dead is by dissection. This is the result of the study of anatomy, which began as early as the beginning of the seventeenth century. By an old statute in England,[3] the body of a person executed for wilful murder was caused to be delivered to the surgeons to be publicly dissected and anatomized; the court could direct that the body be hung in chains, but finally to be dissected.[4] This was the only means, probably, of obtaining human anatomies in England down to 1832. The demand for them became so great that in some cases persons were murdered for their bodies. Professional men had to rely principally on body-snatchers for subjects for dissection,

[1] *Young v. College of Physicians and Surgeons et al.*, 81 Md. 358 (1895).

[2] *Cook et al. v. Walley & Rollins et al.*, 1 Col. App. 163 (1891).

[3] 25 Geo. II., c. 37.

[4] Blackstone's Commentaries, book iv., pages 202, 376.

both in England and America. The bodies of those of whom *post mortem* examinations were of the greatest interest and value to men of science were obtained in spite of almost insuperable difficulties and great expense. The increase of learning and investigation in modern times has made necessary the easier and readier means of obtaining human skeletons; and the law has been statutorily changed to aid science in this respect. Under prescribed circumstances and conditions, the dead bodies of more criminals than heretofore, and of some paupers, can be legally used for dissection.

The law in England against body-snatching was so severe that parties engaged in that business charged great prices for obtaining subjects. This fact occasionally led impecunious people, while alive, to endeavor to sell their own bodies to surgeons, the title to pass upon their decease, but the price to be paid periodically as long as the subject remained alive. This was probably sometimes accomplished, and the agreement duly carried out. The legal objection to such a contract arose from the fact that dead bodies are not property, and cannot be conveyed or contracted for. There have been instances of men in their wills bequeathing their remains for purposes of dissection, but to this the same objection was present. Relatives have rights, also, which even the deceased cannot dispose of.

CHAPTER V.

PROPERTY IN DEAD BODIES.

Dead bodies of human beings are not property in the common meaning of the term, that is, in the commercial sense, and can neither be conveyed, attached, nor taken on execution.[1] Neither can they be inherited.[2] In ancient, and even in modern, times it was the practice in some places to arrest and detain dead bodies for debt; but now all such acts are forbidden.[3]

In the case of *Bogert* v. *City of Indianapolis*,[4] the proposition is laid down "that the bodies of the

---

[1] *Regina* v. *Sharpe*, Dears. & Bell (Eng.) 160 (1857); *Regina* v. *Sharpe*, 40 Eng. L. & Eq. (Eng.) 581 (1857); *Foster* v. *Dodd et al.*, 8 B. & S. (Eng.) 842 (1867); *Williams* v. *Williams*, L. R. 20 Ch. Div. (Eng.) 659 (1882); *Weld* v. *Walker et al.*, 130 Mass. 422 (1881); *Guthrie* v. *Weaver*, 1 Mo. App. 136 (1876); *Hadsell et al.* v. *Hadsell et al.*, 7 Ohio C. C. 196 (1893); *Pierce et ux.* v. *Proprietors of Swan Point Cemetery et al.*, 10 R. I. 227 (1872).

[2] *Matter of Brick Presbyterian Church*, 3 Edw. Ch. (N. Y.) 155 (1837); *Hadsell et al.* v. *Hadsell et al.*, 7 Ohio C. C. 196 (1893).

[3] *Jones* v. *Ashburnham et ux.*, 4 East (Eng.) 460 (1804); *Queen* v. *Fox et al.*, 2 Q. B. (Eng.) 246 (1841); *Pierce et ux.* v. *Proprietors of Swan Point Cemetery et al.*, 10 R. I. 227 (1872).

[4] *Bogert* v. *City of Indianapolis*, 13 Ind. 134 (1859).

dead belong to the surviving relations, in the order of inheritance as property, and that they have the right to dispose of them as such, within restrictions analogous to those by which the disposition of other property is regulated." The court would undoubtedly limit the proposition to the burial and custody of the body prior thereto, and the subsequent preservation and care of the remains, which in fact were the only questions in issue in the case.

There are certain rights, however, which relatives have in the remains of human beings, before they are interred in the earth, which have some of the aspects of property rights, and enable them to be treated as property in certain respects. These rights are those incident to the care and preservation of the remains in a proper and decorous manner. They are somewhat similar to the rights and duties of a bailee in and to a chattel. The persons having charge of bodies hold them in trust; and this trust the court of equity will regulate and protect.[1]

After burial human remains become a part of the earth to which they have been committed, "earth to earth, dust to dust," and the only civil action that can be brought, at common law, for disturbing them, however indecently or impiously they have been treated, is trespass on the soil in which they are buried, *quare clausum fregit*.[2]

The deceased has some authority over the disposition of his own remains, and it is held in America, to a limited extent, can dispose of them by his last

---

[1] *Pierce et ux.* v. *Proprietors of Swan Point Cemetery et al.*, 10 R. I. 227 (1872).

[2] *Meagher* v. *Driscoll*, 99 Mass. 281 (1868).

will.[1] In England, however, it is held that testamentary directions for such disposition cannot be enforced.[2]

[1] *Pierce et ux.* v. *Proprietors of Swan Point Cemetery et al.*, 10 R. I. 227 (1872).
[2] *Williams* v. *Williams*, L. R. 20 Ch. Div. (Eng.) 659 (1882).

CHAPTER VI.

CUSTODY OF DEAD BODIES.

There is only one kind of possession of human remains that any person can have, and that is in the nature of a bailment for the purpose of the funeral services and the burial, and for their preservation and protection both before and after interment; and the right is to possess the body in the same condition it was in when death occurred.[1] This is a trust so sacred that if its duties are neglected, or it is indecently or impiously performed, or abused, the courts will regulate and control its exercise. All those persons who are allied to the decedent by the ties of family or of friendship are interested, and can enforce the trust.[2]

License to enter Premises to take Custody. — A man has a license to enter upon the premises of another for the purpose of assuming custody and removing his wife's remains for the funeral ceremonies and burial, if he has made a demand therefor and been refused.[3]

To whom Custody belongs. — Such custody belongs to those most intimately and closely connected with

---

[1] *Foley* v. *Phelps*, 37 N. Y. S. Rep. 471 (1896).
[2] *Larson* v. *Chase*, 47 Minn. 307 (1891).
[3] *Neilson* v. *Brown et al.*, 13 R. I. 651 (1882).

the deceased by domestic ties, who, of all other persons, ought to render the last sacred services to the remains after death. The universal doctrine is, that if the deceased was married the right of possession belongs to the surviving husband or wife. They are certainly nearer to each other in point of relationship and affection than any other persons, one being the other's constant companion during life, and they, being bound to each other by the closest ties on earth, should have the paramount right to render these last sad services for each other. This is particularly true if they are living together in that relation at the time one of them dies.[1] But the custody of the husband or wife ends with the burial, that being the consummation of the duty.[2]

After the husband and wife, the children next have the right of custody, and that equally.[3]

While it is true that, at common law, only the relatives or friends of the deceased are entitled to the possession of the remains, it is not always so under modern statutes. In some States the legislature has thrust the duty of burial upon utter strangers; and certainly in such cases the statutes must be construed strictly. The persons who have this extraordinary duty are entitled to the custody of the remains until their duty, which is that of burial, is performed, but no longer. A common

---

[1] *Larson* v. *Chase*, 47 Minn. 307 (1891); *Hadsell et al.* v. *Hadsell et al.*, 7 Ohio C. C. 196 (1893).

[2] *Wynkoop* v. *Wynkoop*, 42 Pa. St. 293 (1862).

[3] *Regina* v. *Sharpe*, 40 Eng. L. & Eq. 581 (1857); *Larson* v. *Chase*, 47 Minn. 307 (1891); *Smiley et al.* v. *Bartlett et al.*, 6 Ohio C. C. 234 (1892).

case is that where coroners bury the bodies of strangers and others, upon whose remains inquests have been held. Another case is that, for instance, existing under the laws of Arizona, where a person dies or is found dead upon a sailing vessel, the captain of the craft thus having the duty of the burial of the remains put upon him.[1]

Coroners, for the purposes of an inquest, have the right of possession against every one else, but only for the purposes and for the time of the inquest.

The personal representatives of the deceased, as such, by the American law, have no right to the custody of the remains.[2] The English courts hold the other way, however.[3]

Actions for Deprivation of Custody. — The right of custody of the remains of a relative is guarded so carefully that the law will give substantial damages for the deprivation of such right on the ground of distress of mind. The leading case is that of *Renihan et al.* v. *Wright et al.*,[4] tried in the Indiana courts in 1890. An undertaker, having been engaged by the parents of a deceased girl to keep the remains until they were ready to inter the same, allowed the body to be forwarded to Ohio for burial, without the knowledge or consent of the parents, and refused to inform them as to where the remains were, further than to say, "Your child is in Ohio." The parents

---

[1] Arizona Statutes, Penal Code (1887), § 493, cl. 4.

[2] *Renihan et al.* v. *Wright et al.*, 125 Ind. 536 (1890).

[3] *Queen* v. *Fox et al.*, 2 Q. B. (Eng.) 246 (1841); *Williams* v. *Williams*, L. R. 20 Ch. Div. (Eng.) 659 (1882).

[4] *Renihan et al.* v. *Wright et al.*, 125 Ind. 536 (1890).

brought an action against the undertaker, and recovered heavy damages. The court said: "When the appellants contracted with the appellees to safely keep the body of their daughter until such time as they should desire to inter the same, they did so with a knowledge of the fact that a failure on their part to comply with the terms of such contract would result in injury to the feelings of the appellees, and they must, therefore, be held to have contracted with reference to damages of that character, in the event of a breach of the contract on their part."

CHAPTER VII.

DISPOSITION OF DEAD BODIES.

AFTER the death of the body there must be some disposition made of it. Putrefaction soon begins; and for the sake of the public health, common decency, and the feelings of the relatives and friends of the deceased, the remains must immediately be cared for. Who can do this, who must do it, and where, when, and how it is to be done, are questions that arise for settlement.

THE RIGHT OF BURIAL.

The right of burial is not strictly the right to inter a dead body, or to have one's own body placed in the ground. That is generally understood to be the meaning of the term, because burial is the usual manner of disposing of human remains. But it has a different and a broader construction; it means rather the right of proper and legal disposition, whatever such disposition may be.

Right of the Deceased. — A dead man has rights, the greatest of which is called Christian burial. It is a universal desire of mankind that some service be had over the remains of every person before their final disposition, and that this rite be of a religious character.[1] The word *Christian* is not a denominational term, as here used, but means some proper recognition of the nature of man and the solemnity of his entrance into the world beyond. Christian burial, in this sense, is a term applicable to the Hindu, Mohammedan, and Jew, as well as to the Christian.[2] He has the right to have his remains kept secure from ill treatment, from undue exposure, and from dishonor. All of these rights are, like other privileges, subject to the exigencies of the public, as the necessity for *post mortem* examinations and dissections,[3] exhumation, etc.

A pauper has the same rights in these respects as the man of position and affluence. The person under whose roof he dies cannot cast his dead body out, or expose it to violation, or carry it to the grave uncovered.[4]

But none of these rights can be enforced by the deceased, of course, and neither by his legal representatives after the final disposition of the body, except perhaps so far as they receive directions in the will of the decedent. This leads the courts sometimes to say that a corpse is not capable of rights.[5] Within certain limits, the American law is, that a person may by his last will predispose of

[1] *Queen* v. *Stewart et al.*, 12 Ad. & El. (Eng.) 773 (1840); *Sullivan* v. *Horner, adm'r*, 41 N. J. Eq. 299 (1886); *McCue, adm'r,* v. *Garvey*, 14 Hun (N. Y.) 562 (1878).

[2] *Queen* v. *Price*, L. R. 12 Q. B. Div. (Eng.) 247 (1884).

[3] *Pierce et ux.* v. *Proprietors of Swan Point Cemetery et al.*, 10 R. I. 227 (1872).

[4] *Queen* v. *Stewart et al.*, 12 Ad. & El. (Eng.) 773 (1840); *Wynkoop* v. *Wynkoop*, 42 Pa. St. 293 (1862).

[5] *Queen* v. *Price*, L. R. 12 Q. B. Div. (Eng.) 247 (1884).

his remains;[1] but the English courts hold that no direction of that kind in a will can be enforced.[2]

In England, a person has the right to be interred in the parish cemetery of the parish where he then lived and died.[3]

Right of the Relatives. — The right of burial which the relatives of the deceased have includes the right of separate burial, and the selection of the place of interment.[4] This right can be exercised but once, unless there is sufficient reason shown for making the change of place of interment.[5]

The right of burial ends with the refusal or neglect to exercise it.

The right of the relatives as to the burial and protection of the decedent's body can be controlled in some degree by the terms of his or her last will, if there be one.

In England, the relatives have the right to bury the deceased in the parish cemetery of the parish where he then lived and died.[6] Even Dissenters can bury their deceased children in the churchyard of the Established Church of England.[7]

Relatives of a deceased pauper can have the re-

[1] *Ruggles' Report*, 4 Bradf. (N. Y.) 503 (1856).
[2] *Williams* v. *Williams*, L. R. 20 Ch. Div. (Eng.) 659 (1882).
[3] *Queen* v. *Stewart et al.*, 12 Ad. & El. (Eng.) 773 (1840).
[4] *Sweeney* v. *Muldoon, adm'r*, 139 Mass. 304 (1885); *Smiley et al.* v. *Bartlett et al.*, 6 Ohio C. C. 234 (1892).
[5] *Guthrie* v. *Weaver*, 1 Mo. App. 136 (1876); *Wynkoop* v. *Wynkoop*, 42 Pa. St. 293 (1862).
[6] *Queen* v. *Stewart et al.*, 12 Ad. & El. (Eng.) 773 (1840); *Pierce et ux.* v. *Proprietors of Swan Point Cemetery et al.*, 10 R. I. 227 (1872).
[7] *Kemp* v. *Wickes*, 3 Phil. (Eng.) 264 (1809).

mains disposed of in Christian burial by the authorities of the municipality of which the decedent was a resident.[1]

It is only the near relatives that have this right of burial; and the nearer they are in relationship, the greater their right. The right of the surviving husband or wife, when one of them dies, to bury the body of the deceased, is paramount to that of all other persons.[2] The survivor has a greater interest in the place of interment than the other relatives, as he or she expects to lie there too; and the next of kin will probably have burial lots of their own, it may be in other places.[3] In the case of *Wynkoop* v. *Wynkoop*,[4] the court held that after burial the widow of the deceased had no control over the remains. In its opinion, the court supposes a case where a woman has had three husbands, who all died in wedlock before her, and says that she should not be burdened with the duty and vested with the charge of their three bodies against the expressed wishes of the blood relations and next of kin of each.

Next to the right of the husband and wife is that of the next of kin; and the order in which they have this right is in the order of their relationship or right of inheritance.[5] The class having the first right is that of the children of the deceased; they

---

[1] *Regina* v. *Vann*, 2 Den. C. C. (Eng.) 325 (1851).

[2] *Lakin* v. *Ames et al.*, 10 Cush. (Mass.) 198 (1852); *Durell* v. *Walker et al.*, 130 Mass. 422 (1881); *Larson* v. *Chase*, 47 Minn. 307 (1891); *Hadsell et al.* v. *Hadsell et al.*, 7 Ohio C. C. 196 (1893); *Hackett* v. *Hackett*, 18 R. I. 155 (1893).

[3] *Hadsell et al.* v. *Hadsell et al.*, 7 Ohio C. C. 196 (1893).

[4] *Wynkoop* v. *Wynkoop*, 42 Pa. St. 293 (1862).

[5] *Bogert* v. *City of Indianapolis*, 13 Ind. 134 (1859).

have the right equally as a class, and not individually.[1]

The class next to the children is that of the parents of the deceased.

If these persons or classes are unable to act in the premises because of disability, those next having the right take their places.[2]

When the individuals composing these classes fail to agree as to place of burial, and on other kindred questions, they may appeal to the court of equity to determine the matter, upon all the circumstances.[3]

Right of Personal Representatives. — The executor of the will of the deceased has some degree of right to bury the dead body of his testator; but how extensive that right is, and under what circumstances it may be exercised, are still open questions.[4]

Right of Reinterment. — Generally, the right of burial does not extend to a second burial; that is, it does not allow the party having the right of burial to move the body about from place to place. The remaining right is that of preservation and protection of the remains.[5] However, where good cause is shown, the court will permit a removal; and this permission is not founded on the right of those who have the right of burial, — if it were they would not be compelled to seek authority from the court when the next of kin objected, — but is in the discretion

---

[1] *Regina* v. *Sharpe*, Dears. & Bell (Eng.) 160 (1857); *Smiley et al.* v. *Bartlett et al.*, 6 Ohio C. C. 234 (1892).

[2] *Jenkins* v. *Tucker*, 1 H. Bl. (Eng.) 90 (1788).

[3] *Smiley et al.* v. *Bartlett et al.*, 6 Ohio C. C. 234 (1892).

[4] *Ferrin* v. *Myrick, adm'r*, 53 Barb. (N. Y.) 76 (1869).

[5] *Guthrie* v. *Weaver*, 1 Mo. App. 136 (1876).

of the court. In the case of *Weld* v. *Walker et al.*,[1] where the dead body of a married woman was interred in the lot of a third person, with the husband's consent, given when he was in great distress of mind and on the supposition that the burial was to be merely temporary, the court permitted the husband, though three years had elapsed since the burial, to remove the remains, coffin, and tombstone to his own land, and restrained the owner of the lot from interfering with the removal. A strong argument in favor of such change was the fact that where his wife was buried the husband had no right to care for and adorn her grave, nor to bury any one by her side, or even to have his own remains lie there. But the court said that, where remains have been interred in the lot of another, with the free and full approval of the person having the right of burial, it would not allow them to be disturbed without the consent of the owner of the lot. In the case of *Peters* v. *Peters et al.*,[2] where a woman permitted the body of her deceased husband to be buried in her father's lot, the request for liberty to transfer the remains was not granted. A similar case was that of *Pierce et ux.* v. *Proprietors of Swan Point Cemetery et al.*,[3] where a widow claimed the right to remove the remains of her deceased husband from one place of burial to another, against the wishes of his children. In the case of *Guthrie* v. *Weaver*,[4] the father

---

[1] *Weld* v. *Walker et al.*, 130 Mass 422 (1881).

[2] *Peters* v. *Peters et al.*, 43 N. J. Eq. 140 (1887).

[3] *Pierce et ux.* v. *Proprietors of Swan Point Cemetery et al.*, 10 R. I. 227 (1872).

[4] *Guthrie* v. *Weaver*, 1 Mo. App. 136 (1876).

of the deceased married woman had buried her remains, and it was held that the husband of the deceased had no right to remove them to a place of his own choosing. In the case of *Wynkoop* v. *Wynkoop*,[1] which was a bill in equity brought by a widow against the brother of her deceased husband and his mother, for liberty to remove the remains from the lot of the mother, in which they had been interred, to another cemetery, claiming the right to do so as the administratrix of his estate and as his widow, the court refused its permission.

Legal Nature of the Right of Burial. — The right to inter a corpse is a legal one, and it will be protected by the courts of law.[2]

THE DUTY OF BURIAL.

It has been argued that the personal representatives of the deceased have the duty of his burial; but this cannot be true, as the appointment of an administrator comes after the burial takes place. An executor occupies a position which is a little different from that of an administrator, as he is nominated in the will, and generally knows of his nomination before his testator dies; but even then he has no legal power and authority to act until the will is proved and his nomination is confirmed.[3] One who is named in the will as executor may bury the body of the testator;[4] but it is doubtful if executors have,

---

[1] *Wynkoop* v. *Wynkoop*, 42 Pa. St. 293 (1862).

[2] *Ruggles' Report*, 4 Bradf. (N. Y.) 503 (1856).

[3] *Sullivan* v. *Horner, adm'r*, 41 N. J. Eq. 299 (1886); Blackstone's Commentaries, book ii., page 512.

[4] *Ferrin* v. *Myrick, adm'r*, 53 Barb. (N. Y.) 76 (1869).

at common law, the right, as such representatives, to the custody of the remains.[1] In the case of *Williams* v. *Williams*,[2] the executor acted with the consent of the widow and the son of the deceased testator; and the court decided that in such a case the executor had the right of possession of, and the duty of burying, the body of the deceased. This statement probably arises from the mistaken supposition that, as the legal representatives must finally pay the expenses of the funeral and interment, they are the ones upon whom the duty of burial rests. The duty of burial and the duty of paying the expenses of the funeral and interment are not the same. In many cases, the person upon whom the duty of burial is cast is not obliged to pay the expense of it.

A husband is bound to bury his deceased wife, and a wife to bury her deceased husband.[3] And the duty of burial in such cases ends with the interment.[4]

Children must bury their parents, and parents their children. This is subject to the duty of hus-

---

[1] *Renihan et al.* v. *Wright et al.*, 125 Ind. 536 (1890).

[2] *Williams* v. *Williams*, L. R. 20 Ch. Div. (Eng.) 659 (1882).

[3] *Jenkins* v. *Tucker*, 1 H. Bl. (Eng.) 90 (1788); *Willis* v. *Jones et al., assignees*, 57 Md. 362 (1881); *Durell* v. *Hayward*, 9 Gray (Mass.) 248 (1857); *Cunningham* v. *Reardon*, 98 Mass. 538 (1868); *Weld* v. *Walker et al.*, 130 Mass. 422 (1881); *Sullivan* v. *Horner, adm'r*, 41 N. J. Eq. 299 (1886); *McCue, adm'r,* v. *Garvey*, 14 Hun (N. Y.) 562 (1878); *Estate of John S. Hill*, 4 Dem. (N. Y.) 69 (1886); *Wynkoop* v. *Wynkoop*, 42 Pa. St. 293 (1862); *Pierce et ux.* v. *Proprietors of Swan Point Cemetery et al.*, 10 R. I. 227 (1872). See *Constantinides* v. *Walsh, ex'r*, 146 Mass. 281 (1888).

[4] *Wynkoop* v. *Wynkoop*, 42 Pa. St. 293 (1862).

band and wife to inter the remains of the one who dies first, if the deceased leaves a husband or wife.[1]

When a person upon whom the duty of burial rests is incapable of acting, by disability or absence, the duty falls upon the next one having it, as though the person having the duty first never had it.[2]

Where there are none who claim the right by relationship, it is the duty of those under whose roof a person dies to provide sepulture for the remains. The dead body cannot be cast out, or exposed to violence, or so placed as to offend the feelings or endanger the health of the living. It must be carried to the grave covered, and be given Christian burial.[3]

If any person upon whom the duty of burial is cast is too poor to incur the expense, and has not the means to procure the necessary coffin and service, he is excused from the duty. He is not obliged to borrow money, and thus create a debt for the same. In such a case, and in cases of strangers, etc., the duty is thrust upon the pauper authorities.[4] As the chief justice, Lord Campbell, said in the opinion of the court in the case of *Regina* v. *Vann*,[5] a pauper parent is not obliged to bury his deceased child if he is not financially able; "he cannot sell the body, put it into a hole, or throw it into the river." This was a case where the father of a deceased child had

---

[1] *Jenkins* v. *Tucker*, 1 H. Bl (Eng.) 90 (1788).

[2] *Jenkins* v. *Tucker*, 1 H. Bl. (Eng) 90 (1788).

[3] *Queen* v. *Stewart et al.*, 12 Ad. & El. (Eng.) 773 (1840); *Wynkoop* v. *Wynkoop*, 42 Pa. St. 293 (1862).

[4] *Regina* v. *Vann*, 2 Den. C. C. (Eng.) 325 (1851).

[5] *Regina* v. *Vann*, 2 Den. C. C. (Eng.) 325 (1851).

not the financial means to provide burial for the remains, and he removed the body from his house to a yard in the neighborhood, where it lay decomposing, emitting a strong stench, and constituting a nuisance. He was offered a loan of money wherewith to defray the expense of burial, but he declined to incur a debt. He was indicted[1] for his failure to bury the child, but the court decided that his duty was coextensive with his ability to do so, and that he was not obliged to contract a debt in order to perform that duty.

Many of the American States have prescribed by statute the classes of persons who must care for human remains, and have them properly interred or otherwise legally disposed of. Some of the States make it a criminal offence not to perform the duty, and those who then do it can recover of those who ought to have attended to the burial even as much as three times the amount of the expense of the same.

By the canon law, which prevailed over a large part of Europe, every one was to be buried in the parish churchyard, or in his ancestral sepulchre, if any, or in such place as he might select. A widow was to be buried with her last husband, if she had had more than one. The English law was similar.[2]

MANNER OF DISPOSITION.

In the early barbaric times, when men were nomads to a great extent, the bodies of their dead relatives

---

[1] The indictment is given in full with the report of the case.

[2] *Pierce et ux.* v. *Proprietors of Swan Point Cemetery et al.*, 10 R. I. 227 (1872).

and companions were left as and where they died, without protection from the elements or wild animals and birds. There were no special sanitary reasons why their treatment should be otherwise, and the sentimental influences were too meagre to avail anything. Later, some threw their dead into the sea, and thought that by so doing they had got rid of both ghost and body. Some of the ancient Scythians are said to have eaten their dead. The people of Asian Tibet either buried their dead in the ground, threw them into the river, exposed them to beasts of prey, or cremated them, as the lamas decreed in each instance. In either case the hair was first plucked out from the top of the head, in order, as they professed to believe, to facilitate the transmigration of the soul. The body was then cut into pieces, and the bones broken into fragments by men who made such work their profession.

It is the right of every person to have a decent and conventional disposition made of his remains, and to dispose of them otherwise, as, for instance, to throw them into the street or river, is an indictable offence.[1] The body must not be disgracefully exposed or disposed of. Friends and relatives are not allowed to suffer in silence, and impotently, at the disgraceful and indecent treatment of the dead bodies of their friends when their hearts are wounded with their grief and loss. It is also imprudent to lessen the solemnity of the services of burial, which are the means of deep impressions on the heart for good. This is the universal sentiment throughout Christian countries. Even when death occurs on the ocean,

[1] *Kanavan's Case*, 1 Maine 226 (1821).

and the body must be disposed of there, the consignment thereof to the billows, so far as practicable, is respectful and solemn.[1]

In 1786, the grand duke of Tuscany, Leopold, undertook to abolish the burial system in his territory. All bodies of the dead, without exception, persons of all ranks, conditions, and ages, of both sexes, and with whatever disease they might have died, were brought out from their houses and tumbled into a cart in the night, and conveyed to a pit beyond the city walls, there to putrefy in one loathsome and horrible mass of undistinguishable humanity. On sanitary grounds, some philosophers applauded the movement; but to all natural human feelings it was so abhorrent that the populace rose against it, and it was soon legally annulled.[2]

Burial. — The burial of dead bodies is placing them under or in earth. This was the earliest method of disposing of the dead that at all resembles an intentional disposition. But in the course of time cremation took its place, continuing until the coming of Christ. The belief of the Christians in the resurrection of the body then caused a return to the burial system, which has since prevailed in a greater degree than any other method of disposal.

The manner of burial must be consistent with decency and the preservation of the public health. Any method of burial is valid and proper, and will be permitted at common law, if no nuisance is occasioned thereby.[3] The remains may be placed in

---

[1] *Kanavan's Case*, 1 Maine 226 (1821).

[2] *Gilbert* v. *Buzzard et al.*, 2 Hag. Con. Rep. (Eng.) 333 (1821).

[3] *Bogert* v. *City of Indianapolis*, 13 Ind. 134 (1859).

vaults, or in direct contact with the earth. Anciently there were two kinds of burial, — one above, the other below, the surface of the ground. The latter was the common method, and is so still; the former is obsolete. In burial by the former method the body was laid on the ground, and over it was erected a framework of logs or lumber, or masonry work, producing a tomb-like structure. Over and upon this was piled earth, sometimes to the height of a hundred feet, and having so large a base that some of them covered large areas; in one instance, as much as six acres of ground. These tumuli are found in America, Europe, and Africa, the pyramids of Egypt being but the higher type of such constructions.

Most people have a desire to be buried in their home land. In the declining years of life, one's thought is toward the home of his youth. Later scenes and experiences do not impress him now. However it may be in its operation, this is universally true. The law, in some sense and degree, recognizes this, and provides for the transportation of bodies, sometimes for thousands of miles, for the purpose of burial at home.

A dead body must be disposed of by burial or otherwise before putrefaction sets in. If that can be stayed by freezing or embalming, the time can be lengthened accordingly.

It is a common belief in Eastern countries that the spirits of human beings ought to be allowed three days in which to leave their human tenements after notice has been served upon them by death; and although the people there are accustomed to bury their dead soon after death takes place, they usually leave the tomb open until the third day has passed, or, if they have not left it open, they repair thither on the third day to open it again, so that the spirit may have free egress. Emanuel Swedenborg indorsed this belief.

For three days resuscitation is deemed a possibility; but then decomposition is supposed to take place, as the spirit has departed. When Lazarus died at Bethany, his sisters had hope that he might be raised from the dead by our Lord, but on the fourth day after his death they did not believe it possible. On the third day after the burial of Jesus himself, the women came to anoint his body according to custom; but he was risen; and the prophecy that he should not see corruption was fulfilled, at least in the belief of the people of that time and place.

Even in matter of fact New England it is deemed highly improper, except in cases of dire necessity, as when death has been caused by a very contagious and dangerous disease, to bury a body before the third day after death; while in some localities, as a writer asserts, a window, or an outside door, is still left open meantime for the egress of the spirit, if it should desire to depart earlier. This rule of burial on the third day after death is generally well fixed in the civilized world; though in later times, we presume, there is a common feeling that to bury a corpse within a shorter space of time indicates an improper desire to be rid of the body too quickly. Of course this feeling is the result of those practices of our ancestors and ourselves which have educated us to regard three days as the conventional length of time to retain such bodies in our midst, few persons to-day having a thought of the origin of the practice.

Cremation. — Many people have a natural horror of having their bodies burned after death; but, however it may seem to them, others have a still greater dread of putrefaction, and of the "small cold worm that fretteth the enshrouded form." The only difference between cremation and burial is that one is a quick, and the other a slow, method of accomplishing the same purpose, — that of reducing the body to ashes. Both are subjects upon which no healthy imagination would dwell; but one is inevitable, and while the individual might have a preference for one method over the other, he must remember that the public as such have an interest in the matter. There are many reasons why cremation should be adopted in populous places.

Cremation was very early practised, and before the Christian era it prevailed among the Romans, some of their fine tombs which were made at that time being lined with small recesses for the reception of urns containing the ashes of the dead. In Tibet, the gyalpos are said to have carefully collected the ashes of their incinerated dead, and made them into an image of the deceased.

The teachings of the Christian church brought about a great change in the manner of disposal of human remains. The truths of the resurrection led to a conviction, shallow though it was, that the temple of the Holy Ghost ought not to be disintegrated, but placed in the ground entire, and there await the summons to arise at the last great day. It has been facetiously remarked of the early Christians, that, though they were strongly opposed to the burning of their dead bodies, the same reasons were not urged in opposition to the desire of their enemies to burn them while they were living.

As the matter was wholly ecclesiastical, and the change in the manner of disposition of dead bodies was so complete, the law has never formally forbidden cremation until recently, when one or two States passed statutes to that effect, while others have enacted laws establishing crematories, with all the powers to act in the incineration of human remains that are necessary.

At common law, to burn a dead body, instead of burying it, is not a crime, unless it is so done as to make the operation a public nuisance. The law does not make criminal every act or practice which jars the religious sentiments of the majority of the people.[1]

In the case of *Williams* v. *Williams*,[2] a testator directed his friend to burn his body, and his executors to pay the expense of the same. The executors refused to have this done, and buried the body. The friend fraudulently obtained authority to disinter the body on the pretence of interring it elsewhere. She then burned it, and sued the executors for the amount of the expense. The court held that her action was a fraud on the license board simply, and illegal, and on that ground would not allow her to recover. In the case of *Queen* v. *Price*,[3] a man

---

[1] *Queen* v. *Price*, L. R. 12 Q. B. Div. (Eng.) 247 (1884).

[2] *Williams* v. *Williams*, L. R. 20 Ch. Div. (Eng.) 659 (1882).

[3] *Queen* v. *Price*, L. R. 12 Q. B. Div. (Eng.) 247 (1884).

placed the dead body of his five months' old child in a ten-gallon cask of petroleum, carried it out into a field, and set it on fire. A crowd of people collected, and by application of earth and other means extinguished the flames. The father was arrested and indicted for attempted cremation of his child. The court said that burning was "not highly mischievous or grossly scandalous"; and the defendant was duly acquitted.

Dissection. — Dissection is a means of disposal of dead bodies that arose originally out of necessity, and has since been constantly enlarged by arbitrary law. It has no origin or lodgment in the desires of subjects or friends, few people probably being willing that their remains should be so used.

Physicians and surgeons early found it necessary to the proper understanding of the human frame and system to dissect bodies. Anatomy was practised in England as early as the beginning of the seventeenth century; and the demand for bodies for this purpose became so great, that many people became professional body-snatchers, as they were called, and in some instances murders were brought about for the coveted cash value of the corpse of the dead.

Anatomy is lawful, however much it may shock the sensibilities of many persons, and takes away the right of disposition of the body which every person is assumed to have.[1]

It is an offence at common law to dig up bodies for dissection, because it is the right of the deceased to have his remains disposed of in a proper and decent manner. The law throws around the dead

[1] *Queen* v. *Price*, L. R. 12 Q. B. Div. (Eng.) 247 (1884).

this security, and never allows it to be disturbed except from necessity. Even then the blow falls where it will do the least harm. This security is enhanced by the feelings of the public in regard to such unnatural treatment of the human body, as well as by the sense of outrage on the part of the relatives and friends of the deceased.[1]

Embalming. — Embalming was practised by several peoples, and for a long period of time; but it cannot be presumed that any one now has a wish for such a treatment of his body, although it does seem to be a refinement upon ordinary burial. Its antiquity is very great, antedating the Hebrew captivity in Egypt and the dynasties of the Pharaohs. The purpose of embalming, which gave it preference over any other disposition of bodies, was to save the remains from putrefaction and from insects. Like the Christian peoples, the Egyptians believed in the corporeal resurrection of the "justified" dead; and this method of preservation was deemed essential, as the body must not experience corruption. Embalming in the mummy form was universal and compulsory; and the huge pyramid, the secret pit, and the subterranean labyrinth were made for the resting place of those dried forms. This method of disposal of the bodies of the dead continued to be practised until about the year 700. So far as the books show, the common law never recognized nor opposed this method of disposition.

[1] *Kanavan's Case*, 1 Maine 226 (1821).

CHAPTER VIII.

UNDERTAKERS.

In the early days those persons upon whom the duty of burial was placed had to perform the burial services themselves, or to hire some person to do the work who was as little experienced in and as ignorant of the service as they were. Infractions of proper manner and legal requirements of those portions of the service that related to the public decency and health often occurred, and as often were overlooked on account of the ignorance of the one having it in charge, and the danger of the complainant himself being found guilty of the same kind of misdoing. In the course of time men began to make the conduct of the funeral and burial services of the deceased a vocation. They undertook the entire charge of the remains and services, and were called *undertakers*, by which name they are generally known to-day. The advantages of having the advice and service of those who make the performance of this duty a study and practice are readily appreciated. They understand the mode of procedure and the manner of burial, and have all the means of transportation for bodies and the necessary implements at hand, and skill to use them.

Although a human dead body is not property in the strict sense, yet an undertaker who has such bodies in his possession occupies the position of a bailee in regard to them, and he will be responsible in damages for allowing them to be mutilated or to go out of his possession without legal authority or the consent of those parties having the right to dispose of the same. The leading case on this question is that of *Renihan et al.* v. *Wright et al.*,[1] in which an undertaker was engaged by the plaintiffs, who were the parents of a deceased girl, to keep her remains until they were prepared to inter them. The undertaker allowed the body to be forwarded to another State for burial, without the consent or knowledge of the parents, and refused to inform them as to where the remains were, further than to say, "Your child is in Ohio." The court said: "When the appellants contracted with the appellees to safely keep the body of their daughter until such time as they should desire to inter the same, they did so with a knowledge of the fact that a failure on their part to comply with the terms of such contract would result in injury to the feelings of the appellees, and they must, therefore, be held to have contracted with reference to damages of that character, in the event of a breach of the contract on their part." In this case, several hundred dollars were awarded as damages.

A city regulation that undertakers must be licensed, and that no person other than superintendents of cemeteries or duly licensed undertakers "shall dig any grave, bury any dead body, or open any tomb in

[1] *Renihan et al.* v. *Wright et al.*, 125 Ind. 536 (1890).

any cemetery, graveyard, or other place in the city other than the cemetery, or move from any house or place within the city to any place of burial whatsoever the body of any deceased person," is reasonable and valid.[1] Suitable and trustworthy persons would be thus intrusted with the moving of dead bodies through the public streets of the city with decency and safety; and it would subserve the interest of the city in its public health.

[1] *Commonwealth* v. *Goodrich*, 13 Allen (Mass.) 546 (1866).

CHAPTER IX.

FUNERALS.

Those that have the duty and right of burial have a license to enter upon the premises of others where bodies lie, for the purpose of assuming custody thereof and removing them for the funeral and burial. But if this license is not utilized, it does not extend to a right to enter upon such premises for the purpose of attending the funeral services which others have arranged. A suit for damages, even by a husband who has been refused the privilege of viewing his wife's body, will not lie under such circumstances.[1]

What is proper and legal in the way of funeral ceremonies varies with the religion and enlightenment of the people by whom they are held. A man's death is the most stupendous event of his life, morally as well as materially; and it is but natural that much attention should be paid to it. Lifelong companionships are severed, and objects of love, confidence, sympathy, and support are snatched away. All nations would pay great regard to it, even were the religious element eliminated. Whatever is done to the remains of a deceased human being that is consistent with proper regard and religious belief has always been allowed and pro-

---

[1] *Neilson* v. *Brown et al.*, 13 R. I. 651 (1882).

tected by the law of the time when, the place in which, and the people among whom it is done.

In all ages and parts of the world funeral ceremonies express four purposes: 1. Affection for the dead and grief for the loss; 2. Present interest in and solicitude for their welfare; 3. Fear of them in their present state; and, 4. Affectionate remembrance of them. Primitive peoples show their sorrow in their bereavement by exaggerations of the common expressions of grief, such as groaning and wailing, fasting, neglecting the care of the hair, wearing rags or sackcloth, sitting in ashes, daubing themselves with mud or pigments, wringing the hands, tearing the hair, shaving the head, beating the breast, etc. All believe in a future state, and most of the ceremonies are based on that belief.

Funerals are held either at the residence of the deceased, or in a church, temple, or other sacred place, or at the tomb.

The services immediately precede the burial or other final disposition of the body.

The undertaker or other person having charge of the funeral makes all the arrangements for the services, with the approval of the immediate relatives, if convenient.

The services usually consist of some religious exercises, a sermon, a prayer, and reading from the sacred books of the respective peoples.

The remains are reverently carried to the place of their final disposition on a bier, or, in modern times, in a hearse.

Burial is the most common method of disposition of dead bodies, by high and low, ignorant and cultured, — either beneath the surface of the ground, or under a huge pile of earth and rocks. Coffins and fixed burying places are found among many different races of people, educated and ignorant. Some peoples bury their dead lying at full length, others sitting, and most are particular to lay the body east and west.

The funeral rites of the Christians have always been marked by a high regard for the body, because of their belief in the resurrection. In early times the dead body was swathed in white, placed in a coffin, in which the remains were borne on a bier to the place of interment covered with a pall. It was laid in the grave with the face upward, and evergreen leaves were strewn on the coffin. The funeral and burial occurred in the day-time, in a decorous and solemn manner. Friends were invited to take a parting look. There was also a simple service at the grave. For a while in the fourth century, however, the sacrament of the Lord's Supper was celebrated at the grave.

Natural feelings prompt the use of coffins to keep the remains from present and immediate contact with the earth; and they have now been in common use for a century and a half. They are usually buried with the body, but not always. In the Middle Ages bodies were interred generally without them. In Ireland, until 1818, certain families in Wexford County were in the habit of burying their dead uncoffined. The bodies were carried to the burying place in open coffins with their faces uncovered. The graves were six or more feet deep, and lined with bright green turf from the banks of the river

Slaney. In these green chambers were strewn moss, dry grass, and flowers, and a pillow of the same supported the head of the corpse when it was laid in its last earthly bed. Early in the seventeenth century in England there was a scale of prices for interments, a certain sum for burial with coffin, and a much less sum for burial without coffin. The poor were usually placed in the old oak parish coffin for the purposes of the funeral, or rather taken to the grave in it, and interred in their shroud only. The coffin was then returned to the niche in the wall where it was kept, to remain until it should be again needed. Some of these coffins had been used for two hundred years. They were in use in Durham as early as 1615, and a hundred years later. Burial in the parish coffin was one of the hard things of poverty. Among the many projects of George III. to raise money for the support of his army and navy was that of taxing coffins.

Coffins have been made of all sorts of materials, lead, iron, gold, glass, stone, marble, and clay baked into tiles. The most common and perhaps the earliest used material is wood. The right of burial of dead bodies in coffins made of imperishable materials has been contested in the courts. The privilege of burying in so called imperishable materials is granted, but the authorities are allowed to charge a larger fee therefor, because the occupancy of the ground will necessarily be so much longer. This reason may seem insufficient when the modern cemetery system is fully considered. The right of burial in a churchyard, even now, is not a right to bury a large chest or trunk, either of wood or metal. In the case of

Gilbert v. *Buzzard et al.*,[1] the objection made to an iron coffin was not to its size, as it was smaller on the outside than a wooden coffin, but because it was of a material that would not readily decay. In this case it was a "patent iron coffin," probably locked, made to prevent body-snatching, which was at that time and place uncomfortably common. The use of such coffins is certainly lawful.

Palls are not in common use to-day. In early times in New England the town or parish owned the pall, or the later "burying cloth," which was used by the public. And with the pall pall-bearers have also gone out of fashion, though "bearers," sometimes erroneously called "pall-bearers," are still carriers of the remains.

A "wake," kept by Roman Catholics over the remains of deceased friends, has been recently recognized by the law as a proper service.[2]

The funeral services are of a religious character, being adapted to make a deep impression, and to produce the best effects.[3] They are greatly varied in the exercises, and include the public funeral, held over the remains of a prominent person in a public place, which civic bodies and societies and the public generally attend; the military funeral, conducted in the style and manner prescribed for the burial of the military dead, with the volley fired over the grave and the march of armed soldiers, the drum-beat, and the shrill notes of the fife; and the more private and

---

[1] *Gilbert* v. *Buzzard et al.*, 2 Hag. Con. Rep. (Eng.) 333 (1821).

[2] *McCue, adm'r*, v. *Garvey*, 14 Hun (N. Y.) 562 (1878).

[3] *Kanavan's Case*, 1 Maine 226 (1821).

smaller funerals. Private funerals are also varied in the length and variety of the exercises, and in the decorations. They are generally held in the residence of the deceased, and thus are in the immediate control and charge of the family. Sometimes they are quite ostentatious, the exercises long and varied, and the decorations profuse and costly. Others are extremely simple, flowers are absent, and a short and simple prayer suffices for the religious ceremony. This is not usually owing to poverty, but to the rugged simplicity of the family in their religious faith, believing all ostentation to be sin. It is of such a funeral as this that Whittier wrote "The Friend's Burial":—

> " True as in life, no poor disguise
>   Of death with her is seen,
> And on her simple casket lies
>   No wreath of bloom and green.
>
> " O, not for her the florist's art,
>   The mocking weeds of woe!
> Dear memories in each mourner's heart
>   Like heaven's white lilies blow.
>
> . . . .
>
> " Here organ-swell and church-bell toll
>   Methinks but discord were,—
> The prayerful silence of the soul
>   Is best befitting her.
>
> . . . .
>
> ' From her loved place of prayer I see
>   The plain-robed mourners pass,
> With slow feet treading reverently
>   The graveyard's springing grass."

On the occasion of a burial at sea the people on board the vessel gather round the remains, and a prayer is spoken, the body being then committed to the deep, wrapped in some winding-sheet.

In the early New England days refreshments were served in great abundance at public funerals. These consisted principally of drink. At the funeral of the Rev. Thomas Cobbett, of Ipswich, Mass., who died in 1685, the services being under the auspices of the town, a barrel of wine and a considerable quantity of cider was served. The use of liquors on such occasions has now become unfashionable, but refreshments, served in the form of an ordinary meal, still follow the burial exercises. In this only the mourners participate.

The remains must be borne to the grave covered, the respect due to the memory of the deceased and the feelings and health of the living having proper consideration.[1]

In most countries the relatives of the deceased indicate their bereavement by some change in their apparel. In America and England this is true in regard to the feminine sex, though some men indicate it by wearing crape on their hats. The women wear black clothing, and the widow of the deceased properly wears for a time a black bonnet with a long and heavy black crape veil. Mourning in apparel is generally confined to persons of adult age.

In ancient times it was the practice of the family to give finger rings to the mourners. They were called "mourning rings." The practice became unpopular, and it has not prevailed to any extent for a century.

---

[1] *Queen* v. *Stewart et al.*, 12 Ad. & El. (Eng.) 773 (1840).

Another practice was that of presenting gloves to the mourners and pall-bearers of both sexes. At the funeral of Rev. Thomas Cobbett, mentioned above, there were distributed many dozen pairs. This was a custom quite commonly prevailing until the beginning of this century. Just prior to the year 1800, the gloves were usually made of white leather; subsequently the color was black. Still later, it was the custom of some families to present the officiating clergyman with a pair of black silk gloves.

CHAPTER X.

FUNERAL EXPENSES.

FUNERAL expenses [1] begin as soon as a person dies, with the laying out of the body, and end with its final disposition. They are necessary expenses, both at common law and under all statutes, and have priority over all other claims,[2] being a charge upon the estate of the deceased, and not a debt merely.[3]

Gratuitous Services. — There are claims sometimes made against estates which are either not directly

---

[1] The term "executorship expenses," used in a will, includes the testator's funeral expenses. *Sharp* v. *Lush*, L. R. 10 Ch. Div. (Eng.) 468 (1879).

[2] *Tugwell* v. *Heyman et al, ex'rs*, 3 Campb. (Eng.) 298 (1812); *Sullivan* v. *Horner, adm'r*, 41 N. J. Eq. 299 (1886); *Rappelyea* v. *Russell*, 1 Daly (N. Y.) 214 (1862); *Ferrin* v. *Myrick, adm'r*, 53 Barb. (N. Y.) 76 (1869); *Patterson, ex'x*, v. *Patterson*, 59 N. Y. 574 (1875); *McCue, adm'r*, v. *Garvey*, 14 Hun (N. Y.) 562 (1878); *Gregory* v. *Hooker's adm'r*, 1 Hawks (N. C.) 394 (1821); *Parker, adm'r*, v. *Lewis, adm'r*, 2 Dev. (N. C.) 21 (1828); *Ward & Co.* v. *Jones, adm'r*, Busbee, Law (N. C.) 127 (1852); *Salvo & Wade* v. *Schmidt*, 2 Spears (S. C.) 512 (1844).

[3] *Rappelyea* v. *Russell*, 1 Daly (N. Y.) 214 (1862); *Ferrin* v. *Myrick, adm'r*, 53 Barb. (N. Y.) 57 (1869); *Patterson, ex'x*, v. *Patterson*, 59 N. Y. 574 (1875); *McCue, adm'r*, v. *Garvey*, 14 Hun (N. Y.) 562 (1878); *Gregory* v. *Hooker's adm'r*, 1 Hawks (N. C.) 394 (1821); *Parker, adm'r*, v. *Lewis, adm'r*, 2 Dev. (N. C.) 21 (1828); *Ward & Co.* v. *Jones, adm'r*, Busbee, Law (N. C.) 127 (1852); *Salvo & Wade* v. *Schmidt*, 2 Spears (S. C.) 512 (1844).

connected with the funeral and burial of the deceased, or are furnished by those who should render them gratuitously under the circumstances. A case of this kind was that of *Hewett* v. *Bronson*.[1] A man boarded and made his home with his cousin and her husband for fifteen years. He was one day taken suddenly ill in the street, and died immediately. Not being recognized by those who saw him when he died, his remains were carried to an undertaker's rooms. The man with whom he had lived, missing him, began a search for him, and found his remains in the possession of the undertaker, the public authorities being about to bury them as those of an unknown person. He took charge of the body, and had the funeral at his house. The executor of the will of the deceased paid all the ordinary expenses of the funeral, but refused to pay for the services of the host in searching for his friend, for writing advertisements announcing the funeral and sending them to the newspapers, for procuring a clergyman to perform the funeral exercises, for the use of his house for the funeral and for the deposit of the coffin for a few hours, and for other similar items. Suit was brought to recover for them, but the court held that all this was gratuitous, no money having been spent, and would not allow the claim. A similar case was that of *Lund* v. *Lund*,[2] in New Hampshire, in which a man, who was afterward appointed administrator of the estate, asked the court to allow him in his account for car and coach fare for himself and his wife, and of his sister and

---

[1] *Hewett* v. *Bronson*, 5 Daly (N. Y.) 1 (1873).
[2] *Lund* v. *Lund*, 41 N. H. 355 (1860).

her husband, to attend the funeral of the deceased, who was his brother, and for his time and services in attending the funeral. Touching the propriety of making claim for such services. which true affection would always prompt without any expectation or desire of pecuniary remuneration, the court said: "Economy would suggest that, if mourners must be hired at a funeral, it would be better to procure them as near by as possible, and thus save paying their fare; and it would seem to be much more in accordance with the common notions of propriety, if men must be procured for pay to perform such services, that indifferent strangers be selected rather than brothers and sisters. Tears that flow to order, and are shed for a price, should find no place when men stand around a death-bed or the coffin of parents or children, brothers or sisters."

WHAT IS INCLUDED.

Funeral expenses include the expense of laying out the body, the undertaking, services at the funeral, the cost of the lot, and all expenses of the burial and of marking the grave.

The directions of a testator in his will as to his funeral should be carried out when they are reasonable and proper, and not against public policy, if the estate is solvent. In all other cases it is presumed to be in consonance with his wishes that he be interred in the manner which the custom of his time and place has established.[1] It must be confined to the usage of the neighborhood and period in which

[1] *Rappelyea* v. *Russell*, 1 Daly (N. Y.) 214 (1862); *Hewett* v. *Bronson*, 5 Daly (N. Y.) 1 (1873).

the death occurs, as customs are ever changing, and what may be deemed absolutely essential at one time would be thought absurd at another. The law presumes this, and raises an implied request on the part of the deceased that this be done.[1]

Laying out the Body. — This is the first of the funeral expenses, and is always necessary.

Notice of Death. — The expense of communicating intelligence of the death of the deceased to his family is a part of the funeral expenses, and should be allowed as such. In the case of *Hasler* v. *Hasler*,[2] the deceased committed suicide at a hotel in New York, and a special messenger was sent to Philadelphia to inform the relatives of the deceased, who resided there, of the death. This was shown to be the most prompt means of communication, and was therefore proper and necessary, as the property of the deceased must be secured, adequate preparations made for the transportation and burial of the body, and expenses consequent upon delay avoided.

Transportation of Body. — When a person dies away from home, the expense of the proper transportation of the body thither is a legitimate part of the funeral expenses.[3] It is reasonable to presume that a person wishes to lie among his kindred after his decease, and a request on his part to that end is therefore implied. The only questions that can arise on this rule are, first, whether an insolvent estate should be

---

[1] *Lentz* v. *Pilert*, 60 Md. 296 (1883).

[2] *Hasler* v. *Hasler*, 1 Bradford (N. Y.) 248 (1850). In this case an item of twelve dollars paid for such expenses was allowed.

[3] *Sullivan* v. *Horner, adm'r*, 41 N. J. Eq. 299 (1886); *Hasler* v. *Hasler*, 1 Bradford (N. Y.) 248 (1850).

made to pay for the transportation of the body in such a case; second, as to the means of transportation between the place of death and the place of burial; and, third, the distance the two places are apart. In the case of *Sullivan* v. *Horner, adm'r*,[1] the court allowed such a claim, though the remains were transported from Texas to New Jersey.

The items of such expenses are several in number. One is the cost of the permit of removal and transportation; and if, in order to obtain such permit, it is necessary to secure a certified copy of the verdict of the coroner's jury in a case where the deceased committed suicide, the expense of such copy should be added.[2] Another item is the expense of a person to accompany the remains for the purpose of superintending such transportation.[3]

Shroud. — The shroud or clothing in which the body is interred is necessary, and should be paid for out of the estate.[4]

Coffin. — A coffin is also a necessary article for the interment of the dead, and must be paid for by the estate of the deceased.

Wake. — In the case of *McCue, adm'r*, v. *Garvey*,[5] tried in the New York courts in 1878, a claim of forty-seven dollars for the expenses of a "wake" was allowed.

[1] *Sullivan* v. *Horner, adm'r*, 41 N. J. Eq. 299 (1886).
[2] *Hasler* v. *Hasler*, 1 Bradford (N. Y.) 248 (1850).
[3] *Sullivan* v. *Horner, adm'r*, 41 N. J. Eq. 299 (1886); *Hasler* v. *Hosler*, 1 Bradford (N. Y.) 248 (1850). In the latter case an item of ten dollars paid for such expenses was allowed.
[4] *France's Estate*, 75 Pa. St. 220 (1874). In this case a claim of fourteen dollars paid for grave clothes was allowed.
[5] *McCue, adm'r*, v. *Garvey*, 14 Hun (N. Y.) 562 (1878).

Funeral Services. — The expense of the services at the ordinary funeral is a legitimate part of the funeral expenses. Such is the fee of the officiating clergyman;[1] and probably also the expense of procuring music. The charge of the sexton for tolling the bell possibly may be allowed.

The expense of public funerals is rarely paid for by the estate of the deceased. They are usually under the auspices of some public body, and a large part of the expense is paid by them. The law will not presume, probably, that it is a man's desire to have a public funeral.

Refreshments. — Charges for feasts and entertainment at funerals should not be allowed.

Mourning. — The estate is not to be charged with the expense attendant upon procuring suitable articles of mourning for the immediate family of the deceased.[2] The fact that an executor gives the order for it makes no difference with the rule.[3]

The surrogate court of New York, in the settlement of the *Estate of Alfred Allen*,[4] took a different view of the law. The court said, that, as it was the universal practice for the family of the deceased to wear mourning, and as a change in the wearing apparel was thus rendered necessary, it was a part of the preparation for the funeral, and a mark of proper respect for the dead, and the estate should pay for

[1] *McCue, adm'r, v. Garvey*, 14 Hun (N. Y.) 562 (1878).
[2] *Johnson v. Baker*, 2 C. & P. (Eng.) 207 (1825); *Willis' adm'r v. Heirs of Willis*, 9 Ala. 330 (1846); *Griswold et al. v. Chandler*, 5 N. H. 492 (1831); contra, *Campfield, ex'r, v. Ely et al.*, 1 Green (N. J.) 150 (1832).
[3] *Johnson v. Baker*, 2 C. & P. (Eng.) 207 (1825).
[4] *Estate of Alfred Allen*, 3 Dem. (N. Y.) 524 (1884).

it. The court limited the charge for mourning at the expense of the estate to a proper supply for the family, that is, to such members of it as he was obliged to support in his lifetime. In this estate there were no descendants, and the widow, who had expended for herself fifty-six dollars for mourning, consisting of bonnet, dresses, gloves, veil, cloak, etc., asked to be allowed for it out of the estate, which amounted to several thousand dollars over and above the debts due from it. The claim was allowed. In this case the court was apparently influenced by the situation of the parties and the condition of the estate.

In the case of *In re Wachter's Estate*,[1] in the surrogate's court in New York, the court decided that reasonable expenses incurred by the widow and minor daughter of the deceased in the purchase of mourning attire to wear at the funeral are allowable out of the estate as legitimate funeral expenses. Surrogate Davie said in this decision that not to provide "for the usual and conventional ceremonies in mourning of the dead would seem not only parsimonious, but utterly repugnant to one's conception of justice and propriety."

The true rule is, however, that the estate of a deceased person is not liable for the necessary support, after his decease, of those whom he was bound to support in his lifetime. Mourning is clothing, not procured simply to be worn at the funeral, but for general use; and although it is occasioned by the funeral and worn in response to a conventional decree, it partakes more of the character of ordinary cloth-

[1] *In re Wachter's Estate*, 16 Misc. Rep (N. Y.) 137 (1896).

ing, the better opinion being that it is little more than that, and should not be allowed as a part of the funeral expenses, unless the estate is large and the circumstances peculiar, as in the matter of the *Estate of Alfred Allen.*

The position of the Pennsylvania court on this question is a little peculiar. They will not allow a claim for mourning unless all the next of kin share in it;[1] but will allow it if the widow and children of the deceased receive it alike, though the estate is insolvent.[2]

Mourning Rings. — The estate of the deceased could not ordinarily be charged with the expense of procuring finger rings for distribution among the mourners at the funeral, which was a custom in the olden time. In the English case of *Paice v. Archbishop of Canterbury*,[3] the court allowed a credit in an executor's account of ninety-three pounds, twelve shillings, and sixpence, paid for mourning rings, which were distributed among the relatives and friends of the deceased. The reason of this decision was the language of the will of the deceased. It contained a clause, saying, "and anything not specified I commit to the discretion of my executors." The court held that, as the practice of the times recognized the use of mourning rings as proper, it was a matter within such a discretion of the executors.

Gloves. — Probably an estate was not liable for the

[1] *Flintham's Appeal*, 11 S. & R. (Pa.) 16 (1824).
[2] *Estate of Adna Wood*, 1 Ashmead (Pa.) 314 (182-).
[3] *Paice v. Archbishop of Canterbury*, 14 Ves. (Eng.) 364 (1807).

price of gloves bestowed upon mourners at funerals when such a practice prevailed. Such a charge would certainly not be tenable now.

Portrait. — A claim for the cost of painting a likeness of the deceased, painted after his death by order of the administratrix, cannot be allowed against the estate. In the *Appeal of Ann M'Glinsey, adm'x*,[1] the widow of the deceased, being his administratrix, and having under the law one half of the estate, desired to have a portrait of the deceased as a memorial of him for her own use, and had one painted. She charged the estate with the amount paid therefor, but the court decided that the portrait had no connection whatever with the funeral or burial of the deceased, that it was for her own personal benefit only, and that she, and not the estate, must pay for it.

Bearers. — The expense of bearers can probably be proved against an estate.

Pall and Pall-bearers. — In the time of palls and pall-bearers, the expense thereof was probably a legitimate charge against the estate.

Carriages. — The cost of conveying the family and friends to the place of interment at the time of the funeral is a part of the funeral expenses.[2]

Attendance of Societies at Funerals. — A gratuity given to the members of a society, who paraded at the funeral of the deceased, is not chargeable to the estate. In the *Accounting of M. F. Reynolds, ex'r*,[3]

---

[1] *Appeal of Ann M'Glinsey, adm'x*, 14 S. & R. (Pa.) 64 (1826).

[2] *Donald v. McWhorter*, 44 Miss. 124 (1870).

[3] *Accounting of M. F. Reynolds, ex'r*, 124 N. Y. 388 (1891).

the evidence showed that he had paid to a certain commandery, of which the testator was a member, two hundred and fifty dollars as a gratuity for parading at his funeral. It did not appear that pay had been demanded by the society as a condition of its participation in the funeral. The amount was disallowed as a part of the funeral expenses.

Burial Lot. — The purchase of a burial lot in which to inter the remains of the deceased is always allowable against an estate as a part of the funeral expenses, if he had not already procured one in his lifetime.[1] If he owned a lot, but it is or becomes undesirable at the time of his death, and it is a proper case for the purchase of a new lot, the court will allow the price of the new one as a part of the funeral expenses. Even where a cemetery, in which the deceased was first buried, was undesirable, and it was a proper case for the removal of the remains, the court will allow the cost of a new lot against the estate.[2]

In the case of *Birkholm* v. *Wardell et al.*,[3] a charge of fifteen dollars was allowed for a burial lot. In the *Estate of Alfred Allen*,[4] forty dollars was paid and allowed. In this case the estate amounted to several thousand dollars over and above its indebtedness. In the suit of *Valentine* v. *Valentine*,[5] as against the decedent's next of kin

---

[1] *Birkholm* v. *Wardell et al.*, 42 N. J. Eq. 337 (1886); *Valentine* v. *Valentine*, 4 Redf. (N. Y.) 265 (1880).

[2] *Estate of Alfred Allen*, 3 Dem. (N. Y.) 524 (1884).

[3] *Birkholm* v. *Wardell et al.*, 42 N. J. Eq. 337 (1886).

[4] *Estate of Alfred Allen*, 3 Dem. (N. Y.) 524 (1884).

[5] *Valentine* v. *Valentine*, 4 Redf. (N. Y.) 265 (1880).

three hundred and fifty-one dollars was allowed for a burial lot, the estate amounting to more than thirteen thousand dollars, and most of the kin having assented thereto. But the amount was probably unreasonable, and not to be allowed as against creditors.

The expense of a burial lot is provable against the estate of the deceased, even when the widow who is the administratrix takes the deed of the same in her personal capacity, if she acted in good faith.[1] In such a case, where the funds with which the lot is purchased come from the estate, she should make a declaration of trust, in which she declares that she holds the lot for the children of the deceased in fee, subject to her right of burial therein, and her dower right, and that the children are entitled to all the rights of ownership and burial as if they were the grantees. The widow may be compelled to make such a declaration by a bill in equity; and in such a bill all the children need not join.[2]

The Grave. — Expenditures for digging and filling the grave are a part of the funeral expenses.[3]

Marking Place of Interment. — The term "funeral expenses" includes the cost of suitable headstones, gravestones, and monuments erected to mark the place where the deceased is interred, and also the expense of the inscription thereon necessary to identify the deceased. Such expenses, when reasonable in amount, are to be allowed by the court even

---

[1] *Birkholm v. Wardell et al.*, 42 N. J. Eq. 337 (1886); *Estate of Alfred Allen*, 3 Dem. (N. Y.) 524 (1884).

[2] *Stewart's Appeal*, 81* Pa. St. 323 (1876).

[3] *Polly Fairman's Appeal*, 30 Conn. 205 (1861).

when the estate is insolvent. The representative of an estate is not bound to procure them; it can be settled without doing so. See Chapter XI., entitled MONUMENTS, GRAVESTONES, ETC.

Reinterment. — If the deceased is at first buried in a lot which was hurriedly obtained in the excitement of the occasion without the exercise of due discretion, and it proves to be undesirable, the expense of removal of the body, if it is permitted, is a charge upon the estate as a part of the funeral expenses. In the settlement of the *Estate of Alfred Allen*,[1] which amounted to several thousand dollars more than its indebtedness, the widow of the deceased, who was his executrix, he leaving no descendants, in the confusion and hurry of the death and funeral, had the remains buried in a cemetery that was much neglected, the fences being down, and the ground growing up to briars and infested with woodchucks. Learning, also, that she could not get a good title to the lot in which the remains of the deceased had been interred, she had the body removed to a burial ground that was well kept, a place where she was willing to be buried herself, and the court allowed the expense of the removal in her account.

AMOUNT ALLOWED.

The amount allowed for funeral expenses by the court is dependent principally upon the size and condition of the estate of the deceased, the rank, degree, or position of the deceased being directory to a much smaller degree.[2] Something more than

---

[1] *Estate of Alfred Allen*, 3 Dem. (N. Y.) 524 (1884).
[2] *Jenkins* v. *Tucker*, 1 H. Bl. 90 (1788); *Tugwell* v. *Heyman et*

the mere shroud, coffin, and grave is required, and the last wishes of the dying should be complied with, as to the style and character of the funeral, if the estate is solvent and extravagance is not involved. The law and courts are always more liberal in this respect against legatees and distributees than against creditors.[1] If the estate is insolvent and small, only the cheapest goods and service, and of those only the most necessary, will be allowed.[2] The feelings of the family and friends of the deceased, who would be lavish in the honors which their affection and respect desire to show to the departed, must not be exercised at the expense of creditors. It does not necessarily follow that the remains of a public officer or of a merchant, who have been important and advantageous members of society, should be placed in the rude painted coffin of a pauper.[3] The rule means that the service shall be free from extraordinary and too costly rites and goods.[4] The fact that the deceased had been a public officer does not make a public funeral necessary.[5] An executor or administrator is not at liberty generally to use his

---

al., ex'rs, 3 Campb. (Eng.) 298 (1812); *Brice* v. *Wilson*, 3 N. & M. (Eng.) 512 (1834); *Palmes et al.* v. *Stephens*, R. M. Charlton (Ga.) 56 (1821); *Dampier* v. *St. Paul Trust Co.*, 46 Minn. 526 (1891); *Donald* v. *McWhorter*, 44 Miss. 124 (1870).

[1] *Donald* v. *McWhorter*, 44 Miss. 124 (1870).

[2] *Edwards* v. *Edwards, adm'x*, 2 Cr. & M. (Eng.) 612 (1834); *Palmes et al.* v. *Stephens*, R. M. Charlton (Ga.) 56 (1821).

[3] *Hancock* v. *Podmore, ex'x*, 1 B. & Ad (Eng.) 260 (1830); *Sullivan* v. *Horner, adm'r*, 41 N. J. Eq. 299 (1886); *Estate of G. A. Erlacher*, 3 Redf. (N. Y.) 8 (1877).

[4] *Green* v. *Salmon*, 3 N. & P. (Eng.) 388 (1838).

[5] *Estate of G. A. Erlacher*, 3 Redf. (N. Y.) 8 (1877).

own discretion in this matter. If he pays an extravagant sum for the funeral expenses, and the court will allow but a portion of the amount, he is personally responsible for the difference. The court is the judge of what is reasonable under all the circumstances, aided by a jury.[1] There is an exception to this rule, however, which furnishes latitude to the decision of an undertaker or personal representative. If the appearance of the financial condition of the deceased is such as to warrant the belief that he is not only solvent, but possessed of a considerable estate, and a funeral and burial corresponding to such appearances is secured or furnished in good faith, the court will allow the entire expense.[2] The condition of an estate cannot be determined immediately after death, especially in the case of a business man having varied and extensive interests.

Although the expenditures for the funeral and burial are too large, yet if the personal representatives contract for them with the knowledge and consent of the heirs and other parties then known to be adversely interested, the amount will be allowed. And this is so even against a creditor, if he does not make his claim known to the administratrix until several years after the ordinary statutory limit, and the administratrix and heirs believe that no such claim existed against the estate. The action of *Miller* v. *Morton et al.*[3] was such a case as this.

[1] As to coffins, etc., the general market price, at retail, is the criterion of value. *Kittle* v. *Huntley*, 67 Hun (N. Y.) 617 (1893).

[2] *Stag* v. *Punter*, 3 Atkins (Eng.) 119 (1744); *Estate of Owen Rooney*, 3 Redf. (N. Y.) 15 (1877).

[3] *Miller* v. *Morton et al.*, 89 Hun (N. Y.) 574 (1895).

The expenditures objected to included a burial lot and a monument, the latter costing fourteen hundred dollars, and the value of the estate being thirty-five hundred and forty dollars.

The English court holds that if an administrator, before taking out letters of administration, sanctions an expensive funeral which a relative has ordered, he will be responsible for the full amount of its cost, and can be sued therefor as administrator.[1]

WHO MAY CONTRACT THEREFOR?

Who may contract for the funeral and burial of a deceased person, and bind the estate therefor? Proper burial is necessary, and it is certain that in every instance some one must take the responsibility of having it attended to; and it is not fair nor consistent with justice to make such contractor liable for the expenses that arise therefrom. But every person who takes upon himself such a responsibility cannot escape personal liability. One who intermeddles officiously and incurs expense in the interment of a dead body, when under the circumstances there is no necessity for his action, cannot recover from the personal representatives of the deceased.[2]

The authority to contract in such cases, and at the same time not be personally responsible, arises not from any principle of agency,[3] but from the duty that rests upon certain individuals to see that the

---

[1] *Lucy* v. *Walrond, adm'r*, 3 Bing. N. C. (Eng.) 841 (1837).

[2] *McCue, adm'r,* v. *Garvey*, 14 Hun (N. Y.) 562 (1878); *Gregory* v. *Hooker's adm'r*, 1 Hawks (N. C.) 394 (1821).

[3] *Cunningham* v. *Reardon*, 98 Mass. 538 (1868).

burial takes place.[1] In this sense, personal representatives always have this authority, if practicable; and the rule is so strong that the law raises a promise on the part of executors and administrators to pay the person who, acting within his duty, has arranged for and engaged the funeral, making such representatives the parties having the first right and duty of contracting for such expenditures, or to ratify and adopt if they please the contracts of any other person made for the same purpose, whether such third person has the duty of burial under the circumstances or not.[2] This promise of repayment which the law raises on the part of the personal representatives is of course dependent upon the existence of assets under his control belonging to the estate.[3] Otherwise no promise can be implied to him. If the widow or family of the deceased pays the funeral expenses without objection on the part of the executor, his assent will generally be presumed, and the estate be held liable therefor.[4] In the settle-

---

[1] *Rappelyea* v. *Russell*, 1 Daly (N. Y.) 214 (1862).

[2] *Tugwell* v. *Heyman et al., ex'rs*, 3 Campb. (Eng.) 298 (1812); *Brice* v. *Wilson*, 3 N. & M. (Eng.) 512 (1834); *Rogers* v. *Price*, 3 Y. & J. (Eng.) 28 (1828); *Ambrose* v. *Kerrison*, 10 C. B. (Eng.) 776 (1851); *Sullivan* v. *Horner, adm'r*, 41 N. J. Eq. 299 (1886); *Patterson, ex'x,* v *Patterson*, 59 N. Y. 574 (1875); *McCue, adm'r,* v. *Garvey,* 14 Hun (N. Y.) 562 (1878); *Estate of Susan B. Miller*, 4 Redf. (N. Y.) 302 (1880); contra, *Gregory* v. *Hooker's adm'r,* 1 Hawks (N. C.) 394 (1821).

[3] *Tugwell* v. *Heyman et al., ex'rs*, 3 Campb. (Eng.) 298 (1812); *Rogers* v. *Price*, 3 Y. & J. (Eng.) 28 (1828); *Sullivan* v. *Horner, adm'r*, 41 N. J. Eq. 299 (1886); *Patterson, ex'x,* v. *Patterson*, 59 N. Y. 574 (1875).

[4] *France's Estate*, 75 Pa. St. 220 (1874).

ment of the *Estate of John S. Hill*,[1] the mother, who was also executrix of the will of the deceased, in the presence of the deceased's husband, ignoring him and any rights he had in the matter, gave directions for the funeral to the undertaker, instructing him to spare no expense in the funeral. The instructions were heeded to the letter, and the undertaker charged the expense to her personally. The bill not being paid in due time, he brought suit against her personally, and recovered judgment. She paid it, and took an assignment of it to herself and her co-executor in their representative capacity. It was held that her officious interference in ignoring the rights and duties of the husband relieved both him and the deceased's estate from the obligation imposed upon him and it by law, and that she became personally and primarily liable for the expense.

The husband has the right of contracting for the burial of his wife, and the wife for the burial of her husband.[2]

A parent has the right to order the funeral and burial of his child, and a child of its parent, if the deceased left no husband or wife who will or can exercise their privileges.[3] In the case of *Jenkins* v. *Tucker*,[4] a man went to another country, leaving his wife, who died during his absence, and her father, without the husband's knowledge, paid the expenses of the funeral. The court held that he could recover the amount he paid from the husband.

---

[1] *Estate of John S. Hill*, 4 Dem. (N. Y.) 69 (1886).

[2] *Brice* v. *Wilson*, 3 N. & M. (Eng.) 512 (1834).

[3] *Jenkins* v. *Tucker*, 1 H. Bl. 90 (1788); *Newcombe* v. *Beloe et al.*, L. R. 1 P. & D. (Eng.) 314 (1867).

[4] *Jenkins* v. *Tucker*, 1 H. Bl. (Eng.) 90 (1788).

Brothers and sisters have this right to contract, subject of course to the exercise of such right by those of nearer relationship where such exercise is practicable. In the case of *Rogers* v. *Price*,[1] a resident of England died at the house of his brother in Wales. The brother contracted for the funeral, and the court held the executor responsible to him. In the case of *Bradshaw* v. *Beard*,[2] the defendant's wife voluntarily left him, and resided with her brother, about a mile distant, until her death, which occurred several years later. The brother buried her without any communication from the husband, from whom he was allowed to recover the expense of the funeral. The court said that the case would have had a different aspect if the brother had been guilty of fraud in keeping the knowledge of her death from the husband.

The right of strangers to make such contracts depends upon the circumstances under which the death occurs. It is the duty of every person under whose roof a dead body lies, if no other person exercises such right, to see that it has decent burial.[3] In the case of *Cunningham* v. *Reardon*,[4] the defendant's wife — who was living apart from him for justifiable cause, he having refused to support her or to solicit her to return to him — died at the house where she boarded, and the proprietor of the house paid the expenses of her funeral. He sued the husband, and

---

[1] *Rogers* v. *Price*, 3 Y. & J. (Eng.) 28 (1828).

[2] *Bradshaw* v. *Beard*, 12 C. B., N. S. (Eng.) 344 (1862).

[3] *Cunningham* v. *Reardon*, 98 Mass. 538 (1868); *McCue, adm'r*, v. *Garvey*, 14 Hun (N. Y.) 562 (1878).

[4] *Cunningham* v. *Reardon*, 98 Mass. 538 (1868).

recovered, though no notice of her decease had been given to him. The general rule may be stated to be, that, in the absence of any person whose right it is to bury the remains of a deceased person, or if any such person is present but neglects or refuses to exercise his right, a stranger may contract for the funeral, and bind the estate thereby.[1] A coroner has this right in relation to bodies of strangers found dead.[2]

One having authority to make such a contract becomes by doing so at least a technical creditor of the estate of the deceased.[3]

Notice of Indebtedness.— As a general rule, probably no notice to the party who is responsible to pay the expenses of the funeral and interment of a deceased person is necessary. Such responsibility is an incident attending the relationship of the parties.[4] But where the articles furnished are only a small part of all required, or are furnished by several persons, the fact of the claim and the extent of it should be given to the personal representative, as the assets of the estate are held by him temporarily only; and he might also be subjected to several suits without being at all aware of liability.[5] In many cases the furnishing of many of the articles might be presumed

---

[1] *Walker et al., com'rs*, v. *Sheftall*, 73 Ga. 807 (1884); *Rappelyea* v. *Russell*, 1 Daly (N. Y.) 214 (1862); *Estate of John S. Hill*, 4 Dem. (N. Y.) 69 (1886).

[2] *Walker et al., com'rs*, v. *Sheftall*, 73 Ga. 807 (1884).

[3] *Lentz* v. *Pilert*, 60 Md. 296 (1883).

[4] *Cunningham* v. *Reardon*, 98 Mass. 538 (1868).

[5] *Gregory* v. *Hooker's adm'r*, 1 Hawks (N. C.) 394 (1821); *Parker, adm'r*, v. *Lewis, adm'r*, 2 Dev. (N. C.) 21 (1828); *Ward & Co.* v. *Jones, adm'r*, Busbee, Law (N. C.) 127 (1852).

to be the prompting of love or of feelings of humanity, and even though the articles were known to be furnished, and the persons by whom they were furnished, still the personal representative ought not to be held to know that they were not furnished gratuitously, but were intended to be a charge against the estate of the deceased.[1]

WHO ARE PRIMARILY LIABLE?

By the civil law of ancient Rome, the charge of burial was, first, upon the person to whom it was delegated by the deceased; second, upon the person to whom the property of the deceased was given by will, and, if the property was not so given, then upon the heirs or next of kin in order of relationship.[2]

Under the common law, the general rule is, that he who was responsible for the necessary support of the deceased in his or her lifetime is also liable for his or her burial expenses.[3]

Generally, the estate of the deceased must pay the funeral expenses finally.[4] There is one exception,

[1] *Gregory* v. *Hooker's adm'r*, 1 Hawks (N. C.) 394 (1821).

[2] *Pierce et ux.* v. *Proprietors of Swan Point Cemetery et al.*, 10 R. I. 227 (1872).

[3] *Hapgood* v. *Houghton, ex'r*, 10 Pick. (Mass.) 154 (1830).

[4] *Rogers* v. *Price*, 3 Y. & J. (Eng.) 28 (1828); *Green* v. *Salmon*, 3 N. & P. (Eng.) 388 (1838); *Willeter* v. *Dobie*, 2 K. & J. (Eng.) 647 (1856); *Newcombe* v. *Beloe et al.*, L. R. 1 P. & D. (Eng.) 314 (1867); *Lightbown* v. *M'Myn*, L. R. 33 Ch. Div. (Eng.) 575 (1886); *Cunningham* v. *Reardon*, 98 Mass. 538 (1868); *Constantinides* v. *Walsh, ex'r*, 146 Mass. 281 (1888); *Rappelyea* v. *Russell*, 1 Daly (N. Y.) 214 (1862); *McCue, adm'r*, v. *Garvey*, 14 Hun (N. Y.) 562 (1878); *Freeman, ex'r*, v. *Coit et al.*, 27 Hun (N. Y.) 447 (1882); *Lucas* v. *Hessen et al.*, 13 Daly (N. Y.) 347 (1885); *Estate of John S. Hill*, 4 Dem. (N. Y.) 69 (1886);

however, and that is where one shows by his over-officiousness that he wishes and intends to pay the expenses himself. In such cases the law simply permits him to do so, if no one interested objects.

In order to secure prompt and proper burial there is an implied promise on the part of the executor or administrator of an estate to pay whoever furnishes the services, coffin, etc., for the burial of the deceased out of the funds of the estate, so far as he has assets that can properly be applied to the same;[1] and if he neglects or refuses to do so, he will be personally liable to the undertaker or other person for the amount. This is true, though the service was rendered and the supplies were furnished before the letters of administration were granted. The courts have several times been unsuccessfully asked to make a distinction between executors and administrators in this respect, and an endeavor has been made to show that the executor has an earlier and a broader authority to act. This rule concerning personal representatives applies to public administrators.[2]

This portion of the rule relative to the binding of personal representatives without their knowledge or consent is limited to those services and articles that must be ordered immediately; it does not apply to gravestones, etc.[3]

Moulton, adm'r, v. *Smith, adm'r,* 16 R. I. 126 (1888); *Mease* v. *Wagner,* 1 McC. (S. C.) 395 (1821).

[1] *Lentz* v. *Pilert,* 60 Md. 296 (1883); *Dampier* v. *St. Paul Trust Co.,* 46 Minn. 526 (1891); *McCue, adm'r,* v. *Garvey,* 14 Hun (N. Y.) 562 (1878); *Kittle* v. *Huntley,* 67 Hun (N. Y.) 617 (1893).

[2] *Rappelyea* v. *Russell,* 1 Daly (N. Y.) 214 (1862).

[3] *Samuel* v. *Estate of John Thomas,* 51 Wis. 549 (1881).

The acts of administrators in reference to funeral expenses, so far as they are reasonable in kind and amount, bind the estate of the deceased;[1] and they may be sued personally or in their representative capacity, as they are also personally responsible for the expenses if they contract for them.[2] And where an administrator is allowed in his account for an item of funeral expenses, he thus becomes personally liable to the person who furnished the subject of it.[3]

In a case where an administrator contracted for some headstones to be placed at the grave of the deceased, and he was removed from the trust before he had fully settled for them, the supreme court of New York held that a suit for the balance could be maintained against his successor; though in the court of appeals the decision was reversed, the court standing five to three.[4]

There is a class of cases which some courts hold to be an exception to the general rule, that the estate of a deceased person is primarily liable for his or her funeral expenses. These are the cases where a wife dies, leaving a husband. Some courts hold that the estate of the wife is not liable for her funeral expenses.[5] The general opinion, however, is the

[1] *Ferrin* v. *Myrick, adm'r*, 53 Barb. (N. Y.) 76 (1869).

[2] *Trueman* v. *Tilden*, 6 N. H. 201 (1833); *Ferrin* v. *Myrick, adm'r*, 53 Barb. (N. Y.) 76 (1869); *Ferrin* v. *Myrick, adm'r*, 41 N. Y. 315 (1869).

[3] *Trueman* v. *Tilden*, 6 N. H. 201 (1833).

[4] *Ferrin* v. *Myrick, adm'r*, 53 Barb. (N. Y.) 76 (1869); *Ferrin* v. *Myrick, adm'r*, 41 N. Y. 315 (1869).

[5] *Smyley, adm'r,* v. *Reese et al.*, 53 Ala. 89 (1875); *Lott* v. *Graves*, 67 Ala. 40 (1880); *Staple's Appeal*, 52 Conn. 425 (1884);

other way.[1] The husband is responsible in the first instance, however, to any one who has furnished or ordered the necessary funeral and burial in cases where such acts on the part of the claimant are proper.[2] This is on the general ground that the husband is bound to supply his wife with necessaries, and funeral expenses are within the rule.[3] Of course, if the wife has no estate, or an estate insufficient to pay the expenses, the husband is primarily liable.[4] And a widow is bound by her contract for the furnishing of the funeral of her husband, who has no estate, even though she is a minor.[5] And if the husband, who is the administrator of his wife's estate, dies before settling it, his estate has a lien on hers for the amount of her funeral expenses if he has paid them, and such claim is not barred by the statute of limitations.[6]

The fact that the wife was living separately from

Willis v. *Jones et al., assignees,* 57 Md. 362 (1881); *Sears* v. *Giddey,* 41 Mich. 591 (1879); *Dalrymple* v. *Arnold, adm'r,* 21 Hun. (N. Y.) 110 (1880).

[1] *Willeter* v. *Dobie,* 2 K. & J. (Eng.) 647 (1856); *Cunningham* v. *Reardon,* 98 Mass. 538 (1868); *McCue, adm'r,* v. *Garvey,* 14 Hun (N. Y.) 562 (1878); *Freeman, ex'r,* v. *Coit et al.,* 27 Hun (N. Y.) 447 (1882); *Lucas* v. *Hessen et al.,* 13 Daly (N. Y.) 347 (1885); *Estate of John S. Hill,* 4 Dem. (N. Y.) 69 (1886).

[2] *Jenkins* v. *Tucker,* 1 H. Bl. (Eng.) 90 (1788); *Ambrose* v. *Kerrison,* 10 C. B. (Eng.) 776 (1851); *Bradshaw* v. *Beard,* 12 C. B., N. S. (Eng.) 344 (1862); *Lightbown* v. *M'Myn,* L. R. 33 Ch. Div. (Eng.) 575 (1886); *Staple's Appeal,* 52 Conn. 425 (1884); *McCue, adm'r,* v. *Garvey,* 14 Hun (N. Y.) 562 (1878).

[3] *Constantinides* v. *Walsh, ex'r,* 146 Mass. 281 (1888).

[4] *Estate of John S. Hill,* 4 Dem. (N. Y) 69 (1886).

[5] *Chapple* v. *Cooper,* 13 M. & W. (Eng.) 252 (1844).

[6] *Moulton, adm'r,* v. *Smith, adm'r,* 16 R. I. 126 (1888).

her husband does not affect the liability that the law has placed upon him.[1]

A married woman's estate is bound for her funeral expenses, and not her husband, when she disposes of her estate by will making it subject to the payment of them;[2] and even where she has property under a power of appointment only, and makes a will under the power for the benefit of her creditors, the property being insufficient to pay her debts, and the will containing no charge of debts or funeral expenses.[3]

The funeral expenses of a widow are not a charge upon, nor a debt against, the estate of her husband, who died before her.[4]

In the case of *Sullivan* v. *Horner, adm'r*,[5] a man and his wife and child were all killed at the same time by a collision on a railroad in Texas, and the husband's estate was held to be liable for the funeral expenses of all three. The reason of the decision is not stated, but it probably rested upon the assumption of the theory of the survival of the strongest.

In the case of *Wilson et al.* v. *Staats, ex'r*,[6] the equity court of New Jersey held that an executor was justified in paying the funeral expenses of an indigent sister of the testator, for whose support the income and principal if necessary of a certain sum of money was given by him.

[1] *Ambrose* v. *Kerrison*, 10 C. B. (Eng.) 776 (1851).

[2] *Willeter* v. *Dobie*, 2 K. & J. (Eng.) 647 (1856).

[3] *Lightbown* v. *M'Myn*, L. R. 33 Ch. Div. (Eng.) 575 (1886).

[4] *Lawall et ux.* v. *Kreidler, ex'r*, 3 Rawle (Pa.) 300 (1832); *Mease* v. *Wagner*, 1 McC. (S. C.) 395 (1821).

[5] *Sullivan* v. *Horner, adm'r*, 41 N. J. Eq. 299 (1886).

[6] *Wilson et al.* v. *Staats, ex'r*, 33 N. J. Eq. 524 (1881).

If the deceased was a pauper, and there is no one who is known to be responsible for his burial, the expense must be met by the public out of its treasury, whether it is the parish, town, county, or State.[1]

To whom Credit is given.— An executor is not liable to an undertaker or other person, although he may have sufficient assets of the estate, when the funeral was ordered by and the credit given to another person.[2] But if the person ordering the funeral had a right to do so, he can recover from the estate.[3] Of course the personal representative can ratify the order, and thus constitute the party ordering his agent;[4] or, become liable by promising to pay for the same.[5]

Practice. — A count against a personal representative, charging him with a promise to pay the funeral expenses as such representative, may be joined with a count upon a promise made by the deceased. This promise of the representative may be an actual or an implied one.[6]

If the person who has paid the funeral expenses is a debtor of the estate, and is sued for the debt, he must plead the amount paid for the funeral expenses as a set-off, and not in payment of his debt.[7]

[1] *Queen* v. *Stewart et al.*, 12 Ad. & El. (Eng.) 773 (1840); *Walker et al., com'rs,* v. *Sheftall*, 73 Ga. 807 (1884); *Hadsell et al.* v. *Hadsell et al.*, 7 Ohio C. C. 196 (1893).

[2] *Rogers* v. *Price*, 3 Y. & J. (Eng.) 28 (1828); *Lucas* v. *Hessen et al.*, 13 Daly (N. Y.) 347 (1885).

[3] *Lucas* v. *Hessen et al.*, 13 Daly (N. Y.) 347 (1885).

[4] *Brice* v. *Wilson*, 3 N. & M. (Eng.) 512 (1834); *Lucas* v. *Hessen et al.*, 13 Daly (N. Y.) 347 (1885).

[5] *Brice* v. *Wilson*, 3 N. & M. (Eng.) 512 (1834).

[6] *Hapgood* v. *Houghton, ex'r*, 10 Pick. (Mass.) 154 (1830); *Gregory* v. *Hooker's adm'r*, 1 Hawks (N. C.) 394 (1821).

[7] *Adams, adm'r,* v. *Butts*, 16 Pick. (Mass.) 343 (1835).

The personal representative obtains his reimbursement of the amount which he has paid for funeral expenses by making it an item to his credit in the account of his settlement of the estate with the probate court.[1] He cannot sue himself as such representative for the amount he has thus paid out.[2]

In the case of *Fay* v. *Fay*,[3] the New Jersey court held that, where the personal representative paid a claim for funeral expenses, taking no assignment thereof from the undertaker, and there was no evidence that the payment was otherwise than voluntary, or that it was his intention to keep the claim alive, he was not entitled, by subrogation to the claim, to reimbursement out of the proceeds of the sale of the real estate of the deceased, there being no personal assets.

In the case of *Van Orden* v. *Krouse et al.*,[4] a woman died intestate, leaving an insolvent husband, and no administration was granted on her estate. It was held that the undertaker, who buried her without being requested by any one to do so, furnishing all necessary articles for her burial and interment, could not impress a trust upon her real estate therefor.

MORTUARIES.

Mortuaries were originally gifts made to the minister of the parish, on the death of one of his parishioners, as a sort of amends to the clergy for any tithes, etc., which the deceased had possibly neglected

---

[1] *Gregory* v. *Hooker's adm'r*, 1 Hawks (N. C.) 394 (1821).
[2] *Phillips* v. *Phillips*, 45 Pac. Rep. (Mont.) 221 (1896).
[3] *Fay* v. *Fay*, 43 N. J. Eq. 438 (1887).
[4] *Van Orden* v. *Krouse et al.*, 89 Hun (N. Y.) 1 (1895).

or forgotten to pay. This was not only an ancient English custom, but it prevailed in early times, and perhaps still does, in several countries. In France, a man who in his will failed to provide for them was formerly deprived of Christian burial; but if he died intestate, he would receive the rites of the church, and arbitrators would be appointed to determine the amount that his estate should pay to the minister. Originally, it was customary to bring the mortuary to the church with the remains of the deceased at the time of the burial. As early as the time of Henry III., the practice had become a custom having the effect of law, and such a provision was deemed in England a necessary ingredient of every will. It soon became necessary, in order to prevent undue exaction, fraud, and litigation, to make a law governing the practice. The statute of 21 Henry VIII., chapter 6,[1] was accordingly enacted, reducing mortuaries to a certainty. The statute allowed the application of the custom of paying mortuaries to men who were householders only, and had estates above a certain value.

Probably this practice never prevailed in the United States.

[1] In A. D. 1530.

CHAPTER XI.

MONUMENTS, GRAVESTONES, ETC.

STONES are placed at each end of a grave to mark and define the spot, that it may be known and protected. Gravestones and monuments are erected primarily for the same purpose. They are larger and often more elaborate than they need to be, but something is necessary, and modern usage has made them so common that their cost is allowed as a part of the funeral expenses.[1] They are connected with the burial, and logically have their place with the burial expenses.

This is one of that class of funeral expenses which are not contracted for as others are, because of the necessity of the situation. Tombstones need not be and are not erected until some months after the death takes place; and the personal representatives have ample time to make their own contracts therefor. Indeed, the estate can be settled as well

---

[1] *Van Emon et al.* v. *Superior Court*, 76 Cal. 589 (1888); *Crapo, ex'r,* v. *Armstrong*, 61 Iowa 697 (1883); *Griggs, adm'r,* v. *Veghte et al.*, 47 N. J. Eq. 178 (1890); *Owens* v. *Bloomer, adm'x, et al.*, 14 Hun (N. Y.) 296 (1878); *Porter's Estate*, 77 Pa. St. 43 (1874); *Moulton, adm'r,* v. *Smith, adm'r*, 16 R. I. 126 (1888). See *Sweeney* v. *Muldoon, adm'r*, 139 Mass. 304 (1885).

without procuring them.[1] They are not deemed by the law to be so necessary that they must be erected.

In most countries graves have been marked by monumental stones, generally of the stone slab style. In early times in England, when burials were frequently made in churches, the family of the deceased had the right to erect such slabs in the churches; and when out of door burial became common, similar slabs were placed upright at the head of the grave. The custom has become common, and the plain slab in many instances has given place to monuments of various sizes, shapes, and material, and most elaborate in design and finish.

Public monuments, such as soldiers' monuments, and statues, do not come within the scope of this branch of the law.

WHO CAN CONTRACT THEREFOR?

The personal representative of the deceased is the person to procure the tombstone, and he is the only one who can make a contract therefor which will bind the estate. An administrator can erect a tombstone of more than ordinary value over his intestate's grave, though a step-son of the deceased promised him that it should be done.[2] If the administrator procures them in his representative capacity, the expense will be a charge upon the estate.[3] And though he gave his personal note therefor, the court

[1] *Polly Fairman's Appeal*, 30 Conn. 205 (1861).
[2] *Donald* v. *McWhorter*, 44 Miss. 124 (1870).
[3] *Foley, adm'r,* v. *Bushway,* 71 Ill. 386 (1874); *Lerch, adm'r,* v. *Emmett et al.,* 44 Ind. 331 (1873); *Laird et al.* v. *Arnold, adm'r, et al.,* 42 Hun (N. Y.) 136 (1886).

should if possible hold that it was given as collateral security only.[1]

The Iowa court holds[2] that the widow or heirs of the deceased may ask the court to cause a monument to be erected, if the personal representative refuses; but the Massachusetts court[3] holds to the contrary. Neither of the cases in which this question has been under advisement in the States named is sufficiently definite to settle the position of the courts thereon; and the question is still open. The fact, however, that a personal representative may know that a monument is being erected by the widow of the deceased cannot bind him or the estate. He may be presumed to suppose that she is erecting it on her own account. This she has the right to do, and it would be impertinent in him to object thereto.[4]

Husbands and wives have the first right to erect tombstones over one another's graves.[5] In the case of *Durell* v. *Hayward*,[5] the husband of the deceased caused her remains to be properly interred, and the mother of the deceased, without the husband's knowledge or consent, procured and placed at the grave a memorial stone inscribed as follows: —

IN MEMORY OF
HARRIET M. HAYWARD,
DAUGHTER OF
DAVID AND ALMIRA DURELL,
Born April 11th, 1828,
Died June 13th, 1853.

[1] *Laird et al.* v. *Arnold, adm'r*, 25 Hun (N. Y.) 4 (1881).
[2] *Crapo, ex'r,* v. *Armstrong*, 61 Iowa 697 (1883).
[3] *Sweeney* v. *Muldoon, adm'r*, 139 Mass. 304 (1885).
[4] *Foley, adm'r,* v. *Bushway*, 71 Ill. 386 (1874).
[5] *Durell* v. *Hayward*, 9 Gray (Mass.) 248 (1857).

As soon as the husband discovered the presence of the stone, he caused it to be removed, and a new one to be erected in the same place. The mother then brought an action of tort against the husband for removing the stone. When the husband removed it, he gave no notice whatever to the mother of what he intended to do, or had done, but after the suit was brought he tendered the stone to her, and she refused to receive it. The court held that he had a right to remove any obstruction that was in the way of the exercise of his right to erect a stone, and that he was not liable in this action.

AMOUNT ALLOWED.

A simple and inexpensive gravestone is always proper to be set up, and probably the court would in all cases, whether the estate was solvent or insolvent, allow the cost of it.[1] If the estate is insolvent, the simplest and cheapest tablet should be secured, if any.[2] The executor or administrator has ample time to discover the condition of the estate before he need erect any memorials, and he cannot excuse an excessive outlay on the plea of ignorance. And the same is true of enclosing the cemetery lot.[3] Where the estate is solvent, the administrator ought to consult the heirs, and have the advice and approbation of the court in which the estate is being settled,

---

[1] *Bendall's distributees* v. *Bendall's adm'r*, 24 Ala. 295 (1854); *Cornwell* v. *Deck*, 2 Redf. (N. Y.) 87 (1874); contra, *Estate of G. A. Erlacher*, 3 Redf. (N. Y.) 8 (1877); *Estate of Owen Rooney*, 3 Redf. (N. Y.) 15 (1877).

[2] *Polly Fairman's Appeal*, 30 Conn. 205 (1861).

[3] *Estate of G. A. Erlacher*, 3 Redf. (N. Y.) 8 (1877).

before spending any considerable sum of money for this purpose.[1] In New Hampshire, in 1860, the court held that in cases where the estate amounted to not more than three thousand dollars, from fifteen to thirty dollars only should be allowed for gravestones.[2] In the settlement of an estate in New York, the personal assets of which were two thousand dollars, two hundred dollars was held not to be extravagant for a tombstone.[3] In an estate of eight thousand dollars, in the same State, the expenditure of five hundred dollars for such a purpose was held to be extravagant, and not to be allowed.[4] One hundred and seventy-five dollars was allowed in the settlement of another estate in New York, where the deceased left a widow but no issue, and the estate amounted to several thousand dollars more than the debts due from it.[5] In a case where the deceased left a good estate, and no children, and the widow, who was entitled to one half of the estate, wished to be liberal in honoring her husband's memory, caused a handsome tombstone to be erected over the vault in which his body lay, the claim was allowed.[6] In all cases of solvent estates, in deciding the amount that ought to be expended for a monument or tombstone, due attention and consideration ought to be given to the usages of the region, and the station in life and circumstances of the deceased, as well as to

---

[1] *Polly Fairman's Appeal*, 30 Conn. 205 (1861).
[2] *Lund* v. *Lund*, 41 N. H. 355 (1860).
[3] *Campbell* v. *Purdy*, 5 Redf. (N. Y.) 434 (1881).
[4] *Owens* v. *Bloomer, adm'x, et al.*, 14 Hun (N. Y.) 296 (1878).
[5] *Estate of Alfred Allen*, 3 Dem. (N. Y.) 524 (1884).
[6] *Appeal of Ann M'Glinsey, adm'x*, 14 S. & R. (Pa.) 64 (1826).

the size of his estate.[1] The judge of the court in which the estate is being settled is required to decide as to the amount to be allowed for gravestones, monuments, etc.[2]

Where land is devised subject to a charge for the "just debts and funeral expenses" of the testator, the court is to decide as to the amount to be paid out for such expenses.[3]

Desires expressed orally. — The court will regard an oral expression of a desire on the part of the deceased, as well as one made in a will. In a case where the estate amounted to eight thousand dollars, and was bequeathed to collateral relatives, the testator leaving neither widow nor children, the court allowed a credit of two hundred and ten dollars in the personal representative's account for a marble tombstone, for which the testator had orally expressed a wish.[4]

Directions in Wills. — A testator may provide in his will for suitably marking his grave, and for the adornment and beautifying of the burial places of the dead.[5] Such a direction in a will is not a legacy, but a part of the funeral expenses. If the rights of creditors are affected by such a direction, it has no force as against them.[6] In the case of *Ford, &c.* v.

---

[1] *Crapo, ex'r,* v. *Armstrong,* 61 Iowa 697 (1883); *Griggs, adm'r,* v. *Veghte et al.,* 47 N. J. Eq. 178 (1890).

[2] *Polly Fairman's Appeal,* 30 Conn. 205 (1861); *Crapo, ex'r,* v. *Armstrong,* 61 Iowa 697 (1883).

[3] *Polly Fairman's Appeal,* 30 Conn. 205 (1861).

[4] *Bendall's distributees* v. *Bendall's adm'r,* 24 Ala. 295 (1854).

[5] *Ford, &c.* v. *Ford's ex'r,* 91 Ky. 572 (1891).

[6] *Wood et al.* v. *Vandenburgh et al.,* 6 Paige (N. Y.) 277 (1837).

Ford's ex'r,[1] the Kentucky court held that an appropriation of this kind would be for a charitable purpose if the monument was to be erected in memory of the deceased and his wife, but would not be if it was erected for himself alone. In this case, after providing for the payment of his debts, the funeral expenses of himself and wife (there being no children), costs of administration, and a life estate in all his property given to his wife, the testator directed that all of the estate remaining at his wife's decease be used "for the erection of a monument of the best quality of marble or granite over the graves of my said wife and myself, of such size as the money thus arising will be sufficient to pay for." There was about six thousand dollars remaining in the estate at the decease of the wife. The court upheld the will, upon the ground that it was not a perpetuity.

While it is competent for a testator to devote his whole estate to the erection of a monument to his memory, he must designate his intention in definite terms.[2] In the case of *Emans, ex'r*, v. *Hickman et al.*,[2] in the New York court, where a testator bequeathed his entire estate to his executor "for my funeral expenses and the erection of a monument to my memory," in a certain cemetery, and the estate amounted to twelve hundred dollars, the court decided that there was no expressed intention of spending his whole estate for the purpose named, but only so much as would be suitable to his condition in life. The court held that one hundred and fifty dollars

[1] *Ford, &c.* v. *Ford's ex'r*, 91 Ky. 572 (1891).
[2] *Emans, ex'r*, v. *Hickman et al.*, 12 Hun (N. Y.) 425 (1877).

was a proper amount to be devoted to that purpose, and the balance was ordered to be paid to the heirs.

If a testator directs his executor to erect over his grave a suitable monument, and leaves the selection of the style and expense of it to the executor's discretion, the New York courts hold that the discretion must be exercised according to law and its principles. That is, the executor must have the same judgment as the court, and the effect of the rule is that the executor is left without the discretion given in the will, thus making that portion of it void. The court is still to say what can be allowed against the estate under such a will.[1] In the settlement of the *Estate of Emma J. Luchy*,[2] in the New York courts, where a testatrix directed her executor, in her will, to erect over her grave a suitable monument, leaving the selection of the style and expense of it to his discretion, and he procured a monument costing fourteen hundred and fifty-five dollars, the court refused to allow more than seven hundred dollars for the expense of it in his account. The value of the personal assets of the estate was eleven thousand and ninety-six dollars. The rule is the same when the direction is for the erection of a monument over the graves of both the testatrix and her husband.[3] In the New York case of *Burnett* v. *Noble*,[4] a testatrix directed her executor, in her will, to erect a

---

[1] *Estate of Emma J. Luchy*, 4 Redf. (N. Y.) 95 (1879); *Burnett* v. *Noble*, 5 Redf. (N. Y.) 69 (1880).

[2] *Estate of Emma J. Luchy*, 4 Redf. (N. Y.) 95 (1879).

[3] *Burnett* v. *Noble*, 5 Redf. (N. Y.) 69 (1880).

[4] *Burnett* v. *Noble*, 5 Redf. (N. Y.) 69 (1880).

suitable monument over the graves of herself and her husband, leaving the selection of the style and amount of the expense of it to the discretion of the executor; the executor petitioned the court in which the estate was being settled for liberty to reserve from the assets of the estate the sum of seven hundred dollars with which to purchase the monument. The estate amounted to less than two thousand dollars, and the court would allow but two hundred and fifty dollars for this purpose.

The court in Pennsylvania holds, however, that the discretion is in the executor and not in the court in such cases, and this is apparently the sounder rule. In the settlement of *Ingles' Estate*,[1] a testator directed his executors, in his will, to erect a certain monument described therein, "the cost thereof to be five thousand dollars or thereabouts." The court held that the discretion of the executors was limited to that sum. They purchased one for thirty-five hundred dollars, and the court allowed it. In the case of *Bainbridge's Appeal*,[2] a testator directed his executor, in his will, "to appropriate" the residue of his estate, and the same "to use for and in the erection and construction of a suitable monument at my grave, such as the amount of funds in his hands will warrant." The residue amounted to eight hundred dollars, and the executor procured a monument for seven hundred and fifteen dollars, and that amount was allowed by the court.

Where a testator ordered that five thousand dollars should be expended for the improvement of his burial

---

[1] *Ingles' Estate*, 76 Pa. St. 430 (1874).
[2] *Bainbridge's Appeal*, 97 Pa. St. 482 (1881).

lot in a cemetery, in building a wall around it, and in procuring a monument, etc., the five thousand dollars were exhausted in building the wall, and the court ordered the executor to expend an additional sum for the monument, as the monument was the principal thing for which the appropriation was made, and the estate large.[1]

ALLOWANCE FOR TWO TOMBSTONES.

Where an inexpensive tombstone has been erected over the grave of the deceased, and the body has been subsequently removed to another place, the court may allow the expense of a new tombstone over the new grave.[2] In the settlement of *Howard's Estate*,[2] in the New York courts, the estate being solvent and amounting to over six thousand dollars, the executor was allowed three hundred dollars for such a second tombstone.

EXCHANGE OF MONUMENTS.

In the New York case of the *Accounting of James Frazier et al., ex'rs*,[3] a testator in his will directed his executors to expend not more than two thousand dollars "in repairs" of a cemetery lot. Under that authority a sarcophagus was erected on the lot at an expense of five hundred dollars, and the testator's remains were placed therein. A monument was already on the lot, and the executors exchanged it for a better one; headstones were erected at the graves, and the coping was replaced, at a cost of nine

---

[1] *Porter's Estate*, 77 Pa. St. 43 (1874).

[2] *Howard's Estate*, 3 Del. (N. Y.) 170 (1893).

[3] *Accounting of James Frazier et al., ex'rs*, 92 N. Y. 239 (1883).

hundred and thirty-five dollars. It was held that all these expenditures were within the authority and discretion of the executors, and were rightly included in "repairs."

INSCRIPTIONS.

The earliest epitaphs were Egyptian, and were at first inscribed on coffins. They usually commenced with a prayer to Osiris or Anubis on behalf of the deceased, which was followed by his name, descent, and office. There was no attempt to delineate his character, nor express the feelings of the survivors.

The ancient epitaphs of the Greeks had excellent literary qualities, were strong and often tender in feeling, rich and varied in expression, and usually epigrammatic in form. Their earlier epitaphs were generally written in verse, and the later ones in prose.

The Roman epitaphs are simply a record of facts, the name and age, and sometimes one or two other particulars of the deceased. They began with the letters D. M. or D. M. S., being initials of *Diis Manibus* or *Diis Manibus Sacrum*, and terminated with the name of the person who caused the urn to be made, and a simple statement of his relationship to the deceased.

Most of the inscriptions in England between the twelfth and fourteenth centuries contain an address to the reader in the first person, in which the deceased states his rank, and contrasts it with his doleful state in the grave, warning the reader to prepare for the inevitable change, and closing with a request for his prayers, with an invocation of blessing upon him if he heeds it. In the time of Elizabeth, they began to assume a literary character. English epitaphs represent a greater variety of intellectual and emotional states than those of any other nation.

American inscriptions are generally simple, most of them being only a statement of the name of the deceased, his age, and date of death. Near the close of the eighteenth century a few lines of poetry applicable to the occasion began to be added.

The inscriptions are nearly always more extended than is strictly necessary for the purpose legally intended to be accomplished by the tombstone, but the expense of its engraving will be allowed if it comes within the range of the customary inscription.[1] If the estate of the deceased is insolvent, only the simplest epitaph ought to be allowed to be paid for out of the estate.

In the English case of *Keet* v. *Smith et al.*,[2] a daughter of Rev. H. Keet, a Wesleyan minister of the gospel, was buried in the churchyard of the parish in which he resided, and the incumbent of the parish refused to allow a stone with an inscription describing the deceased as "the daughter of Rev.d H. Keet, Wesleyan Minister," to be erected over her grave, the title of "Rev.d" being objectionable to him. The court held that there was nothing offensive about it, that it was not a title of honor or dignity, that a person prefixing it to his name did not thereby claim to be a person in holy orders, and that ministers of every denomination should have a right to it alike. It is a comparatively modern

[1] *Polly Fairman's Appeal*, 30 Conn. 205 (1861).
[2] *Keet* v. *Smith et al.*, L. R. 1 P. Div. (Eng.) 73 (1875).

title, having been used as such distinctively since the latter part of the seventeenth century only. The inscription was as follows:—

> IN LOVING MEMORY OF
> ANNIE AUGUSTA KEET,
> THE YOUNGER DAUGHTER OF
> THE REV? H. KEET,
> WESLEYAN MINISTER,
> who died at Owston Ferry,
> May 11th, 1874,
> aged 7 years and 9 months.
>
> *Safe sheltered from the storms of life.*

Whoever rightfully erects a tombstone has an action in trespass against any one who erases the inscription.[1] In the case of *Spooner* v. *Brewster*,[2] the parents of the deceased, who was a married woman, erected a tombstone over her grave, having inscribed on its face, "Sacred to the memory of Eleanor Gravenor," and on its back, "The family grave of John and Sarah Spooner," the names of the erectors. The husband of the deceased had a stone-cutter erase the inscription on the back, and the court held the husband liable.

If coats of arms are put upon a monument in a churchyard, neither the ordinary, parson, church warden, nor any other person, can injure them without becoming responsible therefor in damages to the heirs of the deceased.[3]

---

[1] *Spooner* v. *Brewster*, 2 C. & P. (Eng.) 34 (1825); *Spooner* v. *Brewster*, 3 Bing. (Eng.) 136 (1825).

[2] *Spooner* v. *Brewster*, 2 C. & P. (Eng.) 34 (1825).

[3] *Day* v. *Beddingfield et al.*, Noy (Eng.) 104 (1637).

BOUNDS AND FENCES.

Bound stones, curbing, and fences are also to be erected and paid for out of the estate as part of the funeral expenses.[1]

PROPERTY IN MONUMENTS.

The tombstones and monuments erected over graves are chattels, but they cannot be sold or bequeathed. Neither can they be devised. They are in the nature of heirlooms, and descend to the heirs. They are regarded as the property of those who erect them, for the purposes of protection.[2]

[1] *Polly Fairman's Appeal*, 30 Conn. 205 (1861). See *Tuttle, adm'r*, v. *Robinson*, 33 N. H. 104 (1856).

[2] *Spooner* v. *Brewster*, 2 C. & P. (Eng.) 34 (1825).

CHAPTER XII.

PERMITS TO TRANSPORT, BURY, AND EXHUME DEAD BODIES.

A PROPER respect for the quiet repose of the dead, regard for the tender sensibilities of the living, and due preservation of the public health, require that dead bodies should not be transported, buried, nor disinterred, except for good cause and with due care.[1] Public boards are everywhere appointed to regulate and control these services, and every case is decided separately. If the circumstances are proper, permits are issued. These are required, not only to preserve the public health and to prevent contagious diseases, but to detect and punish crime. These purposes plainly show that such requirements are necessarily within the authority of a municipality, in the exercise of its police powers and duties. Ordinances making it a crime either to transport, bury, or exhume dead bodies without such permit are reasonable and valid.[2]

To Transport. — See Chapter XIII., entitled TRANSPORTATION OF DEAD BODIES.

To Bury. — Police powers are always legal and proper, and nothing can be exempt from their con-

---
[1] *Secor's Case*, 13 Leg. Int. 268.
[2] *Graves* v. *City of Bloomington*, 17 Bradw. (Ill.) 476 (1885).

trol. Ordinances compelling procuration of permits to bury before the interment of dead bodies are as binding upon cemetery associations as upon individuals. Chartered rights are not infringed thereby, even though the association was incorporated many years before the ordinance was passed, and even before the incorporation of the city.[1]

When an ordinance says that "every person engaged or concerned in a burial" is responsible for burying a dead body without a permit, it ought not to be so construed as to include all those persons who are present at the interment from motives of sympathy and friendship, and assist therein; but it ought to include "those who cause or procure the burial and are responsible for the expense of it, and those who as a matter of business and for compensation prepare the grave and fill it up after the body has been placed therein."[1]

If the burial ordinances of a city require a physician's certificate of the cause of the death of the deceased to be filed with the proper officer before a burial permit is granted, and a *post mortem* examination is necessary to the determination of the cause of death, the physician who, at the request of the undertaker, is to make the certificate, may perform an autopsy of the remains in a decent and scientific manner, having due regard to the sex of the deceased and the feelings of the family, and without undue exposure, although the relatives do not consent to it.[2] In the case of *Cook et al.* v. *Walley & Rollins et al.*,[2] a woman who lived apart from her husband and chil-

---

[1] *Graves* v. *City of Bloomington*, 17 Bradw. (Ill.) 476 (1885).
[2] *Cook et al.* v. *Walley & Rollins et al.*, 1 Col. App. 163 (1891).

dren suddenly died in a hack while riding with a man other than her husband. The man delivered the body to an undertaker, by whom a physician was requested to make and sign a certificate of her death, its cause, etc. The cause of her death could not be determined without an autopsy, which the undertaker permitted, but which was made without the consent of the family of the deceased. The heirs of the dead woman brought a suit for damages against the undertaker, but the court decided that the action could not be maintained.

If the by-laws of a cemetery association require parties having the right to make interments in its cemetery to procure a permit from its officers before doing so, and they unreasonably and arbitrarily refuse to issue it, they can be compelled to do so by mandamus.[1] In the case of *Mt. Moriah Cemetery Association v. Commonwealth*,[1] the permit was refused because the body was that of a colored woman.

To Exhume. — In Rome, a dead body could not be exhumed except by permission of the Pontifical College; and in the provinces by the permission of the governor.[2]

In the common law countries such permits are now issued in proper cases as a matter of course, under modern statutes.

---

[1] *Mt. Moriah Cemetery Association* v. *Commonwealth*, 81 Pa. St. 235 (1876).

[2] *Pierce et ux.* v. *Proprietors of Swan Point Cemetery et al.*, 10 R. I. 227 (1872).

CHAPTER XIII.

TRANSPORTATION OF DEAD BODIES.

BEFORE the days of railroads, dead human bodies were rarely conveyed to a distance; but now transportation by steam cars is so expeditious and gentle that remains are frequently carried to distant places. Railroads generally require a person to travel with the corpse to superintend its transportation, and charge the same price for the carriage as though the person was alive.

In the Indiana case of the *Lake Erie & Western R. R. Co.* v. *James*,[1] the railroad company refused to transport a body because the permit attached to the box containing the remains failed to state the name of the physician who attended the deceased in his last illness, as required by the rules of the board of health. The majority of the court held that there must be a strict compliance with the rules before the railroad company could be compelled to transport the corpse. Chief Justice Lotz and Justice Reinhard insisted that it was a mere recital, and that the name was not necessary to the validity of the permit, and dissented from the opinion of the rest of the court.

---

[1] *Lake Erie & Western R. R. Co.* v. *James*, 10 Ind. App. 550 (1894).

A railroad company must not be negligent in the transportation of bodies, or delay the same. A wife can recover damages for distress of mind occasioned by the negligence of a railroad company in delaying for one day the transportation of her husband's corpse.[1] But where the railroad company made their contract with a stranger to the family, and the existence of the parents of the dead person was not disclosed to it, the deceased's mother cannot recover for her mental anguish and suffering on account of being deprived of a sight of the corpse, owing to the delay of the company in its transportation. The suffering of the mother could not have reasonably been in the contemplation of the company as a probable consequence of the breach of the contract.[2]

Statutory Regulations. — At common law it was only required that the bodies of deceased persons should be carried in a decent manner, covered from the view of the public, both for the respect of the deceased as well as the feelings of the public, and in such a manner as not to endanger the public health. Statutes have enlarged these duties, and now make necessary the securing of permits or licenses to carry bodies to, from, or through a town, county, or State, as the case requires. These licenses are generally obtained, upon application to the proper municipal authorities, for a nominal fee.

In England the matter of transportation of dead bodies is by statute placed in the hands of the public burial board.[3]

---

[1] *Hale* v. *Bonner et al.*, 82 Texas 33 (1892).
[2] *Nichols* v. *Eddy*, 24 S. W. Rep. (Texas) 316 (1894).
[3] 41 & 42 Vict., c. 52, § 179.

In the United States it is generally treated as local, and is under the control of municipal authorities, being within their police powers and duties.

In Arkansas [1] and Kansas,[2] transfer permits, with proper coupons attached, are issued by local boards of health for the transportation of bodies that are to be carried for burial beyond the limits of the county in which the death occurred, and the coupons are to be detached and preserved by every common carrier, or the person in charge of any vessel, railroad train, or vehicle, to whom such dead bodies are delivered for transportation.

In California, a permit from the board of health or health officer (if such a board or office exists), and from the mayor or other head of the municipal government of the city, town, or county, in writing, must be first obtained to transport a disinterred body through the streets and highways of such city, town, or county.[3]

In Connecticut, the statute provides that no person shall remove bodies from or into the limits of any town in the State otherwise than for immediate burial in the cemetery adjacent to the town in which the person died, unless there is attached to the coffin or case containing such body a written or printed permit, signed by the registrar of deaths in said town, certifying to the cause of death or disease of which the person died; and if such disease or cause of death is shown by the permit to have been cholera, yellow fever, diphtheria, scarlet fever, small-pox, or

---

[1] Digest of Arkansas Statutes (1883), § 490.
[2] Kansas Comp. Laws (1885), page 539, § 3362.
[3] Laws of California, Act of April 1, 1878, § 1.

other pestilential disease, the permit must further certify that the body is enclosed in an air-tight coffin or case hermetically sealed, or has been disinfected, or both.[1]

Dakota gave, by statute, the right to carry bodies through its territory, and to remove therefrom the bodies of the dead dying within it for the purpose of burying the same in other States or Territories.[2]

The Massachusetts statutes provide that no body shall be removed from any city or town until a permit has been issued by the board of health therein, or, if there is none, from the city or town clerk;[3] and that no railroad corporation or other common carrier or person shall convey, or cause to be conveyed, through or from any city or town in the Commonwealth, the body of any person who died of small-pox, scarlet fever, diphtheria, or typhoid fever, until the body has been so encased and prepared as to preclude any danger of communicating the disease to others by its transportation, and the permit for such transportation must be accompanied with a certificate from the board of health of the city, or the selectmen of the town in which the death occurred, stating the cause of death, and that the body has been so prepared.[4]

In New York, the remains of persons dying within the State may be carried out of it for burial else-

---

[1] Statutes of Connecticut (1888), § 113. A heavy fine is placed upon any person signing a permit knowing it to be false, or permitting it to be used, with such knowledge.

[2] Dakota Penal Code, § 350.

[3] Acts of 1893, c. 263, § 2, amending Pub. Sts., c. 32, § 5.

[4] Acts of 1883, c. 124, § 2.

where; and bodies may be carried through the State,[1] a permit being first obtained in all cases.[2] Bodies must not be detained by attachment or arrest on their way to burial.[3] Permits, with proper coupons attached, are issued by local boards of health for such transportation beyond the limits of the county in which the death occurred, and the coupons are to be detached and preserved by every common carrier, or the person in charge of any vessel, railroad train, or vehicle by which such bodies are transported.[4] Bodies carried over railroads and in passenger steamboats on rivers within the State must be enclosed in a hermetically sealed casket of metal or other indestructible material, if the physician's certificate states the cause of death to have been a contagious or infectious disease.[5]

In Ohio, permits from the board of health are required to remove bodies to or from a city.[6] No one lawfully possessed of a corpse for surgical or medical study can remove it beyond the limits of the State, or transport or attempt to transport it, by railroad or other public conveyance, without its being securely enclosed in a box or case suitable for transportation.[7]

[1] New York Code and Laws (1889), page 366, and Penal Code, § 307.

[2] New York Code and Laws (1889), page 1317.

[3] New York Code and Laws (1889), page 366, and Penal Code, §§ 314, 315.

[4] New York Code and Laws (1889), page 1314; Acts of 1880, c. 322, § 7.

[5] New York Code and Laws (1889), page 1324; Acts of 1886, c. 329, § 1.

[6] Ohio Rev. St. (1894), § 2119.

[7] Ohio Rev. St. (1894), § 7035.

In Vermont, no body can be delivered for transportation, or transported, unless it is accompanied by a certificate signed by a physician legally qualified to practise medicine and surgery in that State, or by the attending physician if the death occurred without the State, stating that the deceased did not die of small-pox, Asiatic cholera, typhus fever, yellow fever, diphtheria, or scarlatina. If death occurred from diphtheria or scarlatina, the body must be wrapped in a sheet saturated with a solution of a half pound of chloride of zinc in a gallon of water, or a solution of bichromide of mercury of not less than two per cent strength, and encased in an air-tight zinc-, copper-, or lead-lined coffin, or in an airtight iron casket, and enclosed in a strong wooden box, with the space between the coffin and the box filled with sawdust saturated with one of the above named solutions. The health officer must furnish a certificate of the cause of death, and the undertaker an affidavit as to how the body has been prepared and encased; and the health officer of the town, village, or city to which the body is consigned must consent to its receipt.[1]

[1] Vermont St. (1894), c. 193, §§ 4687–4689.

CHAPTER XIV.

EXHUMATION OF DEAD BODIES.

The law against disturbing the repose of the dead has always been severe. The Franks banished from their society one who unearthed a corpse for the purpose of stripping it, and no one was suffered to relieve his wants, till the relatives of the deceased consented to the resumption of his former position in society.[1]

The law may be briefly stated to be, that, when a body has once been buried, no one has the right to remove it without the consent of the owner of the grave, or of the proper ecclesiastical, municipal, or judicial authority.[2] To do so without due authority is a misdemeanor at common law.[3] The motive with which this is done is no defence to the charge, even though it is laudable in itself.[4] In the case of *Regina* v. *Sharpe*,[5] the son of a deceased woman, without leave from the custodians, entered a burying

---

[1] Blackstone's Commentaries, book iv., page 235*

[2] *Weld* v. *Walker et al.*, 130 Mass. 422 (1881); *Pierce et ux.* v. *Proprietors of Swan Point Cemetery et al.*, 10 R. I. 227 (1872).

[3] *Regina* v. *Sharpe*, Dears. & Bell (Eng.) 160 (1857); *Commonwealth* v. *Cooley*, 10 Pick. (Mass.) 37 (1830); *Kincaid's Appeal*, 66 Pa. St. 411 (1870).

[4] *Regina* v. *Sharpe*, Dears. & Bell (Eng.) 160 (1857); *Regina* v. *Sharpe*, 40 Eng. L. & Eq. 581 (1857).

[5] *Regina* v. *Sharpe*, 40 Eng. L. & Eq. 581 (1857).

ground belonging to a congregation of Protestant Dissenters, and disinterred her corpse, removing and reinterring it in a churchyard with the body of his father. The court held that the mere fact that the defendant acted from praiseworthy motives was no defence, and that relationship gave no right to take a body from the grave where it was buried.

A person may be found guilty of the offence of an unlawful disinterment of a dead body, even though he was not actually present, if, with the intention of giving assistance, he is near enough to afford it if needed.[1]

The matter of regulating the exhumation of the dead, as well as their burial, with a view to sanitary purposes, has been regarded by all civilized nations in all times as a proper subject of local regulation.[2] And this police power can be delegated by the legislature to municipal governments.[3]

The owner of a burial lot in a cemetery, in which he has buried his deceased child, can maintain an action of trespass *quare clausum* against the superintendent of the cemetery for disinterring and removing the remains therefrom to "the charity lot," and there burying them in a grave containing two other bodies; and in giving damages the father's feelings can be considered, if the superintendent acted in wilful disregard or careless ignorance of the father's rights.[4] But where one buries his dead, and erects a monument, on land in which he has no interest

---

[1] *Tate* v. *State*, 6 Blackf. (Ind.) 110 (1841).
[2] *In re Wong Yung Quy*, 6 Sawyer (U. S., C. C.) 442 (1880).
[3] *Kincaid's Appeal*, 66 Pa. St. 411 (1870).
[4] *Meagher* v. *Driscoll*, 99 Mass. 281 (1868).

and no rights, without the consent of the owner and possessor of the premises, the latter can remove the remains and the monument before rights of burial are gained, by adverse possession or otherwise, without being liable to the family of the deceased therefor.[1]

Trouble sometimes arises from burying bodies in the lots of third parties. In such a case, if the owner of the lot refuses to permit the removal of a body thus interred, recourse may be had to a court of equity, but a proper case must be made out there before authority will be granted. In the case of *Weld* v. *Walker et al.*,[2] the body of a married woman was buried in the lot of a stranger, with the consent of her husband, given while in great distress of mind and on the supposition that the burial was merely temporary, and the court of equity permitted the removal of the body and coffin and tombstones to the husband's lot, though three years had elapsed since the burial. The court also restrained the owner of the lot from interfering with such removal. In such a case a strong argument in favor of such a decision is, that where the body was then buried the husband had no right to care for and adorn the grave, nor to bury any one there, nor to have even his own remains lie there. But where a body has been interred in another lot with the free and full consent and approval of the person having the right of burial, the court will not interfere without the consent of the owner of the lot.[3] This rule is

---

[1] *Bonham* v. *Loeb*, 18 So. Rep. (Ala.) 300 (1895).

[2] *Weld* v. *Walker et al.*, 130 Mass. 422 (1881).

[3] *Weld* v. *Walker et al.*, 130 Mass. 422 (1881); *Peters* v. *Peters et al.*, 43 N. J. Eq. 140 (1887).

so because the right of burial can be exercised but once.[1] In the case of *Pierce et ux.* v. *Proprietors of Swan Point Cemetery et al.*,[2] a woman removed the body of her deceased husband from its original place of burial, and claimed that she had the right to do so, as his widow, but the claim was successfully resisted by the children of the deceased. In the case of *Wynkoop* v. *Wynkoop*,[3] a widow buried the body of her deceased husband in his mother's lot in a cemetery, and subsequently desired to remove his body to another cemetery, claiming a right to do so as his administratrix and widow; but the court of equity, whose assistance she sought, held that she had no such right as against the wishes of the husband's brothers, who opposed her bill.

There are several ways in which the removal of bodies become necessary, as where a cemetery is taken for public purposes, or abated as a nuisance, or discontinued as a place of repose for the dead. In the case of *Bessemer Land & Improvement Co.* v. *Jenkins*,[4] the plaintiff had notice that an old cemetery had been discontinued, and that parties were requested to remove the remains of their dead to the new burial ground provided by the defendant in lieu of the old; and on the plaintiff's failure to do so, the defendant removed the remains of the plaintiff's

---

[1] *Guthrie* v. *Weaver*, 1 Mo. App. 136 (1876); *Wynkoop* v. *Wynkoop*, 42 Pa. St. 293 (1862).

[2] *Pierce et ux.* v. *Proprietors of Swan Point Cemetery et al.*, 10 R. I. 227 (1872).

[3] *Wynkoop* v. *Wynkoop*, 42 Pa. St. 293 (1862).

[4] *Bessemer Land & Improvement Co.* v. *Jenkins*, 18 So. Rep. (Ala.) 565 (1895).

child, which were buried therein, to the new burial ground, without his knowledge or consent and without particular notice that it was to be done. Suit was brought for disturbance of the remains, but the court held that the defendant was not liable.

If a place of burial is taken for public purposes, the next of kin of those buried therein may claim to be indemnified for the expense of removing and suitably reinterring the remains.[1]

A corpse is not property, and therefore not a subject of larceny. Grave clothes and other articles buried with it are property, however, and those who illegally exhume and carry them away may be indicted therefor at common law.

An indictment for feloniously removing a body from the grave for the purpose of dissection and sale, with a count for feloniously receiving a dead body, knowing it to have been feloniously disinterred, need not allege that the body was that of "a human being," and "a graveyard in the town of Bristol, Ontario County," is a sufficient description of the cemetery.[2] If the indictment alleges the cemetery to be the property of a certain religious parish, it need not be proved.[3]

Indignities offered to human remains in improperly and indecently disinterring them are grounds of an indictment, whether they were buried in consecrated or unconsecrated ground.[4]

---

[1] *Ruggles' Report*, 4 Bradf. (N. Y.) 503 (1857).
[2] *People* v. *Graves*, 5 Parker (N. Y.) 134 (1860).
[3] *Commonwealth* v. *Cooley*, 10 Pick. (Mass.) 37 (1830).
[4] *Foster* v. *Dodd et al.*, 8 B. & S. (Eng.) 842 (1867).

CHAPTER XV.

CEMETERIES.

The word *cemetery* primarily means a sleeping place. It was first applied to burying grounds by the early Christians. Cemeteries were at first not connected with churches, but after a few centuries of the Christian era had passed prominent or saintly persons of the parish began to be interred within the church. No person could or can be buried in a church without the consent of the rector, unless the owner of a manor-house prescribed it. This practice of burying in churches was connected, some say, with the custom of praying for the repose of the souls of the dead. If this is so, it may be the reason why interments were made in the earth in the open area around the church, a practice which began about the year 750, and was brought to America by our English ancestors in the seventeenth century.

In treating this subject, it ought to be ever borne in mind that cemeteries are not the property of one generation alone, either of the departed, or of the living, but of both, and of future generations as well.

TOMBS.

In the ancient days caves were much in demand as depositeries of the bodies of the dead. The first recorded instance of a transfer of real estate is that of the cave of Machpelah in the end of Ephron's field, which Abraham bought of Ephron for the burial of Sarah.[1]

All the great roads leading into Rome are bordered on both sides, for a considerable distance, with rows of tombs; and indeed this is true of all large Roman towns.

By the Roman law there were two kinds of tombs, or rather two kinds of ownership of or right to use them. One was called *familiaria*, or such tombs as any one of the family had a right to be buried in, and the other *hereditaria*, which were for the builder and his heirs.[2]

Anciently, it was the custom to have tombs in churches. The owners of such tombs had no interest in the land, and could not prevent a sale of it together with the church building, and the law is the same still. Neither could the owners prevent the removal of the remains of the dead from the tombs, when required by law, as when it became a nuisance; and this is so even when the owner of such a tomb has devised real estate to the church society in trust "for keeping said tomb in good and decent repair."[3] Burials in tombs are liable to police regulations, the same as burials in the earth.[4]

If a man purchases a lot in a cemetery on which

[1] Genesis, chapter xxiii.

[2] *Pierce et ux.* v. *Proprietors of Swan Point Cemetery et al.*, 10 R. I. 227 (1872).

[3] *Sohier et al.* v. *Trinity Church et al.*, 109 Mass. 1 (1871). Under the Trinity Church, in Boston, which this action concerned, there were seventy-four or more tombs.

[4] *Sohier et al.* v. *Trinity Church et al.*, 109 Mass. 1 (1871).

to build a tomb, a vault, or similar construction, and obtains an absolute grant in fee simple to him and his heirs forever, it would seem that it ought to be perpetual, subject of course to police regulations. Abraham's purchase of the cave of Machpelah, "for a possession of a burying place," was of this permanent character. There was Sarah buried, and also himself, and Isaac and Rebecca; there Jacob buried Leah, and while sojourning in Egypt, and about to die, he made his son Joseph swear to remove his body to that sepulchre of his fathers, which was done through extreme labor and a generation of wandering in the wilderness.[1]

The sale of a lot in a cemetery on which to build a tomb carries with it a suitable right of way to it, and the purchaser has the right to remove in a reasonable manner structures built by vote of a parish, which owned the cemetery with the town, in such a way as to obstruct the entrance to the tomb.[2] In the case of *Lakin* v. *Ames et al.*,[2] the son of the owner of the tomb, who was a widow, under an implied license arising from the relationship of the parties, it being a family tomb, and from the exigency of the occasion, for the purpose of depositing therein the corpse of another son of the owner, tore down a shed which obstructed the passage to it, and was acquitted by the court for the act.

Receiving Tombs. — A great many cemeteries have large tombs in which to place bodies temporarily while awaiting interment. In the winter season,

---

[1] *Matter of Brick Presbyterian Church*, 3 Edw. Ch. (N. Y.) 155 (1837).

[2] *Lakin* v. *Ames et al.*, 10 Cush. (Mass.) 198 (1852).

when the ground is either frozen to a great depth, or it is covered by a large amount of snow, at the North, such receptacles are almost absolutely necessary. When spring opens, the bodies are removed to their respective graves.

These tombs are usually built of brick or stone, and above ground, being ordinary buildings in the manner of their construction.

In Germany, and also in many places in England, there are dead-houses, or similar institutions. Their purpose, however, is more extensive than that of the American tombs, being, first, to remove the bodies as soon as possible from the close dwellings of the living, and, second, to avoid premature interment. They are well ventilated, kept at even temperature, and each body rests on a bier. On one of the fingers is placed a ring connected by a light cord with a bell which hangs outside in the warder's room. A chapel, in which funerals are held, is in the same building. The use of such dead-houses is voluntary.

WHAT CONSTITUTES A CEMETERY.

A cemetery is a plot of land set apart for the burial of the dead; and is created by the act which sets it apart, marking and distinguishing it from the adjoining land, with some avowal or act showing that it is intended for the purposes of burial.[1] A religious consecration of the lot as a cemetery is such an act.[2]

---

[1] *Concordia Cemetery Association* v. *Minnesota & Northwestern R. R. Co.*, 121 Ill. 199 (1887).

[2] *Beatty et al.* v. *Trustees of German Lutheran Church of Georgetown*, 2 Peters (U. S.) 566 (1829).

Where a corporation is empowered to buy and sell land for burial purposes, the acceptance of a deed to it of a certain described lot of land does not give the plot described and conveyed the character of a cemetery. It does not become a cemetery technically until the corporation lays it out and opens it to the public for burial purposes. A part or the whole of it may be laid out, in the discretion of the corporation, but if the whole is not laid out only that portion having its peculiar attributes and character becomes a cemetery. It frequently happens that, in order to get the land desired, a larger tract has to be purchased. When this is done, the undesirable part can be sold without any of the characteristics of cemetery land attaching to it.[1]

In some States, cemeteries are defined by statute, as in California, where "six or more human bodies being buried at one place constitutes the place a cemetery."[2]

As burial of dead bodies is the only possession, when claimed and known, necessary ultimately to complete ownership of the easement so as to render it inheritable as long as it is enclosed as a burial place, or even without enclosure as long as gravestones stand marking the place as a burial ground, the possession is, from the nature of the case, necessarily, and therefore, in legal contemplation, actual, adverse, and notorious. Moreover, there cannot be an actual ouster of possession by an intruder, nor running of the statute of limitations in his favor,

---

[1] *Concordia Cemetery Association* v. *Minnesota & Northwestern R. R. Co.*, 121 Ill. 199 (1887).

[2] California Political Code, § 3106.

while such gravestones stand there indicating by inscriptions the previous burial of another.[1]

ESTABLISHMENT OF CEMETERIES.

An addition to a cemetery may be regarded as the establishment of a new burial ground, no matter how the old part is held.[2]

Where the reasons are sufficient, a cemetery company can lay out new avenues and replot their burial ground, even against the wishes of the lot owners, who have made interments therein. The cutting of a new street through a cemetery by the public authorities is a good reason for replotting, lots being cut through and destroyed. New lots, however, should be given to those lot owners who have suffered from the change. And this is true even when the lots have been conveyed in fee.[3]

In some jurisdictions, statutes provide that cemeteries shall not be established within a certain distance of dwelling-houses. Such statutes are reasonable and valid. More concerning this prohibition will be found in Chapter XVI., entitled PROHIBITION OF CEMETERIES.

KINDS OF CEMETERIES.

The kinds of cemeteries are principally dependent upon the government that controls them.

Interments in Churches. — After two or three centuries of the Christian era had elapsed, some of the

---

[1] *Hook, &c.* v. *Joyce,* 94 Ky. 450 (1893).

[2] *Edwards et ux.* v. *Stonington Cemetery Association,* 20 Conn. 466 (1850).

[3] *Root et al.* v. *Odd Fellows Cemetery Co.,* 148 Pa. St. 494 (1892).

leading lights of the church, or men prominent in the region, were buried in the church, generally of their own parish. Persons of pre-eminent sanctity were at first the only ones thus interred, but the rule was sometimes disregarded in favor of some who had more influence than Christianity, but who desired to be reckoned among the faithful of the Lord. The custom is by no means obsolete. Our forefathers in America brought the same idea from the mother country; and in several places in the Atlantic States such tombs can still be seen. Under the Trinity Church in Boston, as late as 1871, there were as many as seventy-four tombs, and in that year they were abolished by a special act of the legislature, on the ground that the continuance of the cemetery was dangerous to the health of the public.

At common law, the only person who could license interments in a church was the parson, the frank tenement being in him only. Neither the ordinary nor church wardens had authority in the matter.[1]

Churchyards. — As the space for tombs within and under the churches became less after interments in churches had become comparatively common, men less memorable were buried in enclosed places not connected with the church edifices. Churchyards began to be used as cemeteries in England about the year 750, through the influence of the Archbishop of Canterbury, Cuthbert, the idea coming from Rome. The space of ground adjoining the church was carefully enclosed and solemnly consecrated by religious

---

[1] *Day* v. *Beddingfield et al.*, Noy (Eng.) 104 (1637).

services, and appropriated to the burial of those who were, or who should thereafter be, entitled to attend religious services within the respective churches, without payment for the privilege of burial or the solemnization of the interment at common law, except when the payment of such a fee had been the immemorial custom of the parish;[1] and the law courts will compel burial if it is refused therein.[2] A child of a Dissenter cannot be refused burial by a minister of the Church of England;[3] but a nonresident of the parish should probably not be buried in the churchyard without the consent of the parishioners or church wardens whose parochial rights are thus invaded.

Christians were glad to lie so near the sacred place of worship, where the living would be apt to see their graves, and think of them when they resorted thither for public worship.

In Scotland, the obligation of providing and maintaining a churchyard rests on the heritors of the parish. They are its guardians, together with the kirk session. The right of burial appears to be strictly limited to parishioners, although some think that any person dying in the parish has the right of interment therein. The parishioners have no power of management. If the heritors fail to pro-

---

[1] *Dean and Chapter of Exeter's Case*, 1 Salk. (Eng.) 334 (1707); *Andrews v. Cawthorne*, Willes (Eng.) 536 (1745); *Gilbert v. Buzzard et al.*, 2 Hag. Con. Rep. (Eng.) 333 (1821); *Pierce et ux. v. Proprietors of Swan Point Cemetery et al.*, 10 R. I. 227 (1872).

[2] *King v. Coleridge et al.*, 2 B. & Ald. (Eng.) 806 (1819); *Ex parte Blackmore*, 1 B. & Ad. (Eng.) 122 (1830).

[3] *Kemp v. Wickes*, 3 Phil. (Eng.) 264 (1809).

vide due accommodations, the presbytery of the church may interfere to compel it to be done, but they have no further jurisdiction.

In England, and generally by the canon law, a wife was to be buried with her last husband, if she had more than one; and on a permanent change of residence a man lost his right to be buried in the churchyard of the place of his former residence, and gained a right in the new parish.[1]

A parishioner is not entitled as of right to bury his dead relative in the churchyard as near to his ancestors as possible,[2] nor in any other particular part of the yard, or in a vault;[3] this is in the discretion of the rector and church wardens.[4] This discretion must be exercised in each case as it arises,[5] and the right of exclusive burial in any part of the yard, or in a particular vault under the church, for a person and his family or friends, cannot be given by the rector by parol or by deed.[6] If the rector has attempted to do this and a certain vault has been assigned, no action will lie for the disturbance of the same.[7] In the case of *Nevill* v. *Bridger*,[8] it was held, however, that a vicar, being

---

[1] *Pierce et ux.* v. *Proprietors of Swan Point Cemetery et al.*, 10 R. I. 227 (1872).

[2] *Fryar* v. *Johnson*, 2 Wilson (Eng.) 28 (1755); *Pierce et ux.* v. *Proprietors of Swan Point Cemetery et al.*, 10 R. I. 227 (1872).

[3] *Ex parte Blackmore*, 1 B. & Ad. (Eng.) 122 (1830).

[4] *Ex parte Blackmore*, 1 B. & Ad. (Eng.) 122 (1830).

[5] *Bryan* v. *Whistler*, 8 B. & C. (Eng.) 288 (1828).

[6] *Bryan* v. *Whistler*, 8 B. & C. (Eng.) 288 (1828); *Bryan* v. *Whistler*, 2 M. & R. (Eng.) 318 (1828).

[7] *Bryan* v. *Whistler*, 2 M. & R. (Eng.) 318 (1828).

[8] *Nevill* v. *Bridger*, L. R. 9 Ex. (Eng.) 214 (1874).

the freeholder of the church and churchyard,[1] can make a special contract by virtue of which a non-parishioner could be buried in a particular vault in the church.

The law of Scotland hesitates to give churchyards the ordinary incidents of real estate; and it is not certain to whom the soil belongs. The questions that arise are those relating to the title to the minerals in the ground, and to the grass and other products of the surface of the yard.

Notwithstanding the sacred nature of the consecrated churchyard, a right of way may be obtained through it by prescription.

It was at common law a crime for a person to draw a weapon, even in self-defence, in a consecrated churchyard.[2]

Denominational Cemeteries. — This class of cemeteries consists of those that have been established and are controlled by some one denomination of the Church. The Catholic denomination is that which has most of such cemeteries, but they are not wholly confined to that sect. Among all denominations the burial of the dead is associated with the belief in the resurrection of the body, and funeral rites are based thereon. Even the rude forefathers of New England were "each in his narrow cell forever laid" in a burying ground established and controlled by a particular ecclesiastical sect, whose minister said a last prayer at the uncovered grave.

It is lawful for the owner of land to sow it with whatever seed he pleases; so land owned by a

---

[1] *Spooner* v. *Brewster*, 3 Bing. (Eng.) 136 (1825).
[2] *Day* v. *Beddingfield et al.*, Noy (Eng.) 104 (1637).

church can just as legally be appropriated by it for the burial of a certain class of persons, upon such conditions as it sees fit. And it is perfectly legal to limit the class to those only who agree with the church in its religious beliefs.[1] And where persons have been buried there with the understanding that only people of their particular creed or faith shall be laid there, no one can acquire a right to disturb their peace by placing therein the remains of those who, under the laws of the church, have no right of sepulture therein.[2] If the trustees of a denominational cemetery give a deed conveying a larger right than the rules of the church allow, it is valid only so far as such rules permit. The payment of money for the right of burial cannot affect it.[3]

Churches may sell lots and rights of burial in their cemeteries, or they may establish free burying grounds, which are the same as other free burial grounds, except that they are confined to the people of their denomination.[4]

In the case of *Wall Street M. E. Church* v. *Johnson et al.*,[5] real estate was bought by a church, the deed being made to three persons as "managers and trustees in trust" for the church, for cemetery purposes, and two years later the trustees were incorporated with the common consent of the grantor,

---

[1] *Application of St. Bernard & St. Lawrence Cemetery Association*, 58 Conn. 91 (1889).

[2] *Dwenger et al.* v. *Geary et al.*, 113 Ind. 106 (1887).

[3] *Price et al.* v. *M. E. Church et al.*, 4 Ohio 515 (1831).

[4] *Antrim et al., tr's,* v. *Malsbury et al.*, 43 N. J. Eq. 288 (1887).

[5] *Wall Street M. E. Church* v. *Johnson et al.*, 140 Ind. 445 (1894).

grantees, and church authorities, the powers of the original grantees being enlarged thereby. It was also provided that they might make rules for the selection of their successors; and in pursuance thereof they passed a by-law authorizing the board of trustees of the church to fill all vacancies that might occur in the cemetery board, which was done, and there was acquiescence on the part of the church authorities for more than fifty years. A suit was brought by the church against the cemetery trustees to quiet the title to the cemetery, to restrain them from interfering therewith, and for the appointment of new trustees, and to compel an accounting to them. The court held that the suit would not lie; although in a proper action, alleging their trusteeship, the defendants might be required to give an account of their proceedings.

National Cemeteries. — These are cemeteries created and existing by acts of Congress; such as the Gettysburg battlefield, cemeteries connected with soldiers' homes, military posts, etc.

State Cemeteries. — California and some other States have burying grounds existing by statute and controlled by the State, some of which are connected with State institutions.

Public Cemeteries. — Public cemeteries are those burying grounds which are under the sole control of towns and cities. They may be established by dedication, gift, purchase, or condemning of land therefor. Whichever way or manner it comes, the city or town gets the title thereto. A public cemetery is proved to be such by the use and occupation of the ground for that purpose. If it has once acquired that character, it does not lose it by mere disuse. It is not necessary to show that it was extensively used by many persons and families, but that burials have been made by others than the owners of the soil, and as of right. The jury can consider the number of the graves, the inscriptions, and the circumstances generally, in determining the question.[1] In the case of *Commonwealth v. Viall*,[2] the cemetery was an ancient neighborhood burial ground, originally private, but by the owners gradually permitting the neighbors to be buried there it was made public. It was finally taken by the town as a public cemetery, and the court held that it was such.

Where land for a cemetery was originally granted to a parish, and subsequently the parish was incorporated into a town, the title to the cemetery passes to the town. It then remains the property of the town until, by the creation of a new parish in the town, it becomes separated into two distinct corporations, having diverse and independent powers. The cemetery then reverts to the parish, unless in the mean time it had been appropriated, as it could be, to the use of the town in its municipal capacity, by a vote or other positive act of the town when there was no parish.[3]

Although township trustees have bought land for a cemetery, they still have a discretion as to its use, and they cannot be compelled to put it to that use,

---

[1] *Commonwealth v Viall*, 2 Allen (Mass.) 512 (1861); *Commonwealth v. Wellington*, 7 Allen (Mass.) 299 (1863).

[2] *Commonwealth v. Viall*, 2 Allen (Mass.) 512 (1861).

[3] *Lakin v. Ames et al.*, 10 Cush. (Mass.) 198 (1852).

if they find it unsuitable or inconvenient, before interments are made therein.[1]

In the case of *Fay et al.* v. *Inhabitants of Milford*,[2] a cemetery belonging to a town became unsuitable, and a lot of land was bought and opened as a new one. The town voted to give "in exchange lots therein free of expense to those holding lots in the old" one, and adopted by-laws which constituted the selectmen a board of trustees to take charge of the new ground, authorizing them to sell lots, and providing that "all money received by the trustees for the lots in this cemetery, and the avails of all lots received in exchange for said lots, shall constitute a fund for the purpose of defraying the expenses of repairing and improving the avenues, walks, and public grounds of the cemetery." Deeds were given subject to these by-laws, "and to any by-laws, rules, or regulations which said town may hereafter adopt." Provision was also made for the removal of the dead. A portion of the old burial ground had been divided into lots, many of which had been sold or otherwise set apart to inhabitants of the town. Some portions of the old cemetery were appropriated to other purposes, and others sold, lots being exchanged as above. The court decided that there was nothing to indicate a contract with any of the lot owners that the "avails" should be applied to the use and improvement of the cemetery, or that the fund should be set apart as a trust fund.

Free Cemeteries. — Free burying grounds are those where lots are not sold, and where one may bury his

---

[1] *Christy* v. *Whitmore et al.*, 67 Iowa 60 (1885).

[2] *Fay et al.* v. *Inhabitants of Milford*, 124 Mass. 79 (1878).

dead where he will, so long as he does not encroach upon rights already gained by others. It would be a trespass for one to fence into his lot a part of another person's lot in which interments had been made; or to obstruct a roadway necessary for its use. If persons, after having taken a lot, move away before they have had occasion to make interments therein, another may take it; but if a person has staked out a lot and entered into possession of it, and not abandoned it, he thereby obtains such an interest and possession as will enable him to defend it against an appropriation by another.[1]

Where the members of a church bought land, and dedicated it as a free burying ground under the control of the discipline of the church, and the members of a family were buried in one end of a large lot, the widow of one of the persons buried in the lot cannot be prevented from being interred by his side, she being a member of the church. In such a cemetery the first occupant cannot be crowded out, and if there is room his wife can be placed by his side.[2]

Cemetery Associations. — The civilization of the age demands that the resting places of our dead shall be made attractive and beautiful, and for this end legislatures generally have power to incorporate persons into associations.[3] Many ancient burial places have been much neglected, and left without

---

[1] *Pierce* v *Spafford*, 53 Vt. 394 (1881).

[2] *Antrim et al., tr's, v. Malsbury et al*, 43 N. J. Eq. 288 (1887).

[3] *Town of Lake View* v. *Rose Hill Cemetery Co.*, 70 Ill. 191 (1873).

the care appropriate to them. Private associations find it for their interest to employ skill, not only in the laying out of their grounds, but in the permanent care of them, and this produces places delightful to the natural sentiments of the living.[1]

Private cemetery corporations cannot as a rule obtain land for cemetery purposes under the power of eminent domain. It must be purchased, and the title obtained by deed in the ordinary manner. See Chapter XVII., entitled ACQUIREMENT OF CEMETERY LANDS, for the different opinions concerning the taking of lands by cemetery corporations under the right of eminent domain.

There is nothing in the nature or objects of a cemetery association which necessarily impresses upon it a trust character. Where the charter provides that the association, out of the proceeds of the sales of lots, shall "keep the grounds in repair and in good order," it is not charged with the care and repair of lots sold to individuals for burial purposes, and the surplus revenue belongs to its members.[2] Neither have lot owners the right to inspect the books of the association.[3] They are not members of the association unless elected under the charter, when it provides that a certain number of persons shall constitute it, and they are to be elected by the association.[4]

---

[1] *Commonwealth* v. *Viall*, 2 Allen (Mass.) 512 (1861).

[2] *Bourland et al.* v. *Springdale Cemetery Association et al.*, 158 Ill. 458 (1895); *Bourland* v. *Springdale Cemetery Association*, 42 N. E. Rep. (Ill.) 86 (1895).

[3] *Bourland et al.* v. *Springdale Cemetery Association et al.*, 56 Ill. App. 298 (1894).

[4] *Bourland et al* v. *Springdale Cemetery Association et al.*, 56

Where the members of the corporation were to be the owners of lots, which were to be conveyed to them in fee, and to be occupied only as burial places, with the use of the walks, etc., subject to the rules, etc. of the association, and with a further agreement that the proceeds of the sales of lots should belong to the corporation, the proceeds go to the corporators individually, and not to the corporation; and if the corporation sell the area not already sold and conveyed, on condition that the grantee assumes all the debts of the corporation, it does not constitute the grantee a trustee of the corporation.[1]

In the case of *Bennett et al.* v. *Culver*,[2] land was conveyed to a cemetery association in consideration of ten dollars and an agreement to pay the grantor and his heirs and assigns forty dollars for each lot of four hundred square feet, and in the same proportion for a larger or a smaller lot, which the association should dispose of as a place of burial, and three dollars for every grave opened, until all the land should be sold for cemetery purposes only, the grantor and his heirs and assigns being entitled to the grass, wood, and other produce of the soil of all parts of the land which might remain unsold until all such land should be sold and have interments therein, and in case of non-fulfilment, the right to all lots in which no interments had been made was

---

Ill. App. 298 (1894); *Bourland* v. *Springdale Cemetery Association*, 42 N. E. Rep. (Ill.) 86 (1895).

[1] *N. Y. Bay Cemetery Co.* v. *Buckmaster et al.*, 49 N. J. Eq. 439 (1892).

[2] *Bennett et al.* v. *Culver*, 27 Hun (N. Y.) 554 (1882).

to revert to the grantor and his heirs and assigns, the court held that he and his heirs were entitled to possession until all the lots were sold and interments actually made therein, and that ejectment would lie to recover possession from a purchaser at a sale under an execution issued upon a judgment recovered against the association.

A shareholder can petition the court of equity for the appointment of a receiver to wind up a cemetery association, when it has failed to maintain the cemetery in proper condition, unlawfully increased the stock, misapplied the trust funds, and closed, altered, and changed the drives.[1]

Private Cemeteries. — In many places in New England it was the early practice to bury one's dead upon his own estate, perhaps because the people were so scattered that it was too far to convey the remains to any central cemetery. When the estate was sold, the burial lot was generally excepted from the operation of the conveyance, or it was reserved to the grantor and his heirs.[2]

However unwise in some respects it may have been to bury the dead, or build tombs in which their remains were placed on the land of the family, it was certainly legal to do so.[3] It is just as lawful to do so as it is to plant seed, but no nuisance must be caused thereby.[4]

[1] *Houston Cemetery Co. et al.* v. *Drew et al.*, 36 S. W. Rep. (Texas) 802 (1896).

[2] *Pierce et ux.* v. *Proprietors of Swan Point Cemetery et al.*, 10 R. I. 227 (1872).

[3] *Barnes* v. *Hathorn*, 54 Me. 124 (1866).

[4] *Application of St. Bernard & St. Lawrence Cemetery Association*, 58 Conn. 91 (1889).

These family tombs or burying places, as they are usually called, are in disfavor with the law, because the title to lands in America changes owners so frequently that soon no one is left in the region who is sufficiently interested in the burying ground to care for and protect it. Large cemeteries from their size will be looked after and kept attractive for generations after private family lots have been encroached upon, destroyed, and forgotten.

Where a deed reserves to two or more persons the right to use a graveyard, one who has been interfered with, or obstructed in the exercise of his right, can maintain an action for damages occasioned by such interference or obstruction, without joining with him others not affected thereby.[1]

Where a deed executed by an attorney in fact reserves to his descendants the use of a graveyard for burial purposes, such reservation is void, and vests no interest in the son of such attorney, he being a stranger to the deed.[1]

Where a deed excepts "a small lot reserved for a burying ground, two poles square, around the graves where William Hodge and his grandchildren are now buried," with no further description of the lot reserved, the law will fix the boundary of the reserved lot, by making the graves which were there when the conveyance was made a common centre, and extending the lines equally each way until an area of two poles square is laid off.[2]

---

[1] *Herbert* v. *Pue*, 72 Md. 307 (1890).
[2] *Hodge* v. *Blanton*, 38 Tenn. 560 (1858).

CHAPTER XVI.

PROHIBITION OF CEMETERIES.

The establishment or further use of cemeteries may be prohibited by State or municipal authority upon proper grounds. Statutes of this kind must have a general application throughout the State in order to be valid.[1]

Prohibition of Establishment of Cemeteries. — A statutory provision, that no cemetery shall be laid out within a certain distance of a dwelling-house, does not prohibit the taking of a dwelling-house and the land on which it stands, as the design of the statute is not to compel people to live near a cemetery, as such association might be disagreeable and the market value of their property be diminished thereby. If the dwelling-house is thus taken, none of the evils that the statute was passed to prevent can occur, because by taking the land the destruction or removal of the house must follow.[2] Under such a statute, the distance is to be measured from the house itself, and not from its curtilage.[3]

---

[1] *Philadelphia* v. *Westminster Cemetery Co.*, 162 Pa. St. 105 (1894).

[2] *Crowell* v. *Londonderry*, 63 N. H. 42 (1884).

[3] *Wright* v. *Wallasey Local Board*, L. R. 18 Q. B. Div. (Eng.) 783 (1887).

On the question whether a municipal government has the right to pass an ordinance prohibiting in advance the opening of any cemetery in the town without permission of certain officials, some of the courts hold that it cannot, because cemeteries are not nuisances. The South Carolina court holds that a city can by ordinance prohibit the establishment of new burial grounds within the limits of the city if such power is within the statute and the powers of the city charter, and that such a statute is constitutional.[1]

Prohibition of Further Use of Cemeteries. — When a legislature has incorporated a cemetery association, it cannot subsequently take away the franchise without cause. The State can regulate interments for the prevention of injury to the health of the people residing in the neighborhood of the cemetery, whether the cemetery is incorporated or not. They can always exercise their police powers. But when a particular burial ground was the subject of the statute, in the case of *Town of Lake View* v. *Rose Hill Cemetery Co.*,[2] the court was divided on the question. The majority held that the legislature must find reasons for the exercise of such police powers, and that they could not act arbitrarily. The minority held that the legislature must be presumed to have found proper grounds for its action, such as the nearness of Chicago and the rapidity of its growth, and that the court had no right to

[1] *City Council of Charleston* v. *Wentworth Street Baptist Church*, 4 Strob. (S. C.) 306 (1850).
[2] *Town of Lake View* v. *Rose Hill Cemetery Co.*, 70 Ill. 191 (1873).

inquire into the legislature's act when it is a police regulation, and relates to the protection of the health, comfort, and welfare of the community. In this case the act objected to was one fixing the boundaries of a cemetery ten years after the incorporation of the cemetery company.

Boards of health have large discretionary powers, but they must not act fraudulently or through caprice.[1]

[1] *Upjohn* v. *Board of Health et al.*, 46 Mich. 542 (1881).

CHAPTER XVII.

ACQUIREMENT OF CEMETERY LANDS.

There are at least four ways in which lands for cemetery purposes may be acquired:—1. By Prescription; 2. By Dedication; 3. By Conveyance; and, 4. By Right of Eminent Domain.

BY PRESCRIPTION.

An easement of the right of burial may be acquired and perfected by prescription; and such right, once gained, cannot be defeated even by the owner of the soil, but will pass to the heirs at law of the deceased by descent. In the case of *Hook, &c.* v. *Joyce*,[1] the only child and heir of a person thus buried caused tombstones to be placed at the graves of such person and her husband and son, who were also buried there, the lot to be enclosed and otherwise cared for, and was afterwards herself buried there.

In the case of *Zirngibl* v. *Calument & C. Canal & Dock Co.*,[2] possession of a few square feet of land by a grave, having a fence around it, in a small tract of land used as a general burial ground, had been had for twenty-nine years, and the court held that it created a title by prescription to the space

---

[1] *Hook, &c.* v. *Joyce*, 94 Ky. 450 (1893).

[2] *Zirngibl* v. *Calument & C. Canal & Dock Co.*, 42 N. E. Rep. (Ill.) 431 (1895).

enclosed by the fence, but not to the forty-acre lot in which the burial ground was located.

The ordinary rule of prescription does not, however, run against the easement of a burial lot.[1]

BY DEDICATION.

Land may be dedicated to the use of a cemetery.[2] No deed or other writing, nor any particular form or ceremony or proceeding, is necessary to pass the title to the easement.[3] It may be made by an oral statement to that effect; but it need not be made to any person legally capable of taking a conveyance otherwise than in trust.[4] It may also arise from the conduct of the owner, and the acts of those who rely thereon, so that while the title remains in the owner of the fee he will be estopped to interfere with the use which he has occasioned.[5]

Where the owner of land buried his own child therein, and subsequently allowed his neighbors to use the lot as a burial ground, declaring that he had devoted it to such a use, and the subsequent owner recognized it as a burial place and did not object to its being so used, it is sufficient evidence of the dedication of the lot to the public for a cemetery.[6]

---

[1] *Hook, &c.* v. *Joyce*, 94 Ky. 450 (1893).

[2] *Hunter* v. *Trustees of Sandy Hill*, 6 Hill (N. Y.) 407 (1844).

[3] *Davidson* v. *Reed et al.*, 111 Ill. 167 (1884); *Hicks et al.* v. *Danford et al.*, 47 Ind. 223 (1874); *Hunter* v. *Trustees of Sandy Hill*, 6 Hill (N. Y.) 407 (1844).

[4] *Redwood Cemetery Association* v. *Bandy et al.*, 93 Ind. 246 (1883).

[5] *Redwood Cemetery Association* v. *Bandy et al.*, 93 Ind. 246 (1883); *State* v. *Wilson*, 94 N. C. 1015 (1886).

[6] *Davidson* v. *Reed et al.*, 111 Ill. 167 (1884).

The staking off a lot of land by the owner, with the intention of donating it to the use of the neighborhood for a burial ground, and setting stones at the corners, and allowing a neighbor to select a lot therein, in which the neighbor buried his wife's remains, all of which occurred at or about the same time, and subsequently permitting about twenty-five other bodies to be buried there, are facts which conclusively prove the dedication.[1]

A dedication also legally takes place where the public had used a certain lot of land for burial purposes with the permission of the occupant only for a certain time, and afterward with the consent of the new owner of the fee; and the same effect was had upon an additional lot, which was also allowed by the owner to be used for that purpose, though in the latter instance something was said about paying for the land used, but no payment had been made.[2]

The giving of the privilege of burial to neighbors promiscuously, although the owner of the soil continues to use it as private property, except so as not to disturb the graves and their appurtenances, is a sufficient dedication at common law.[3]

The following statement of facts also conclusively shows the dedication of the premises for burial purposes. The original proprietors of Kansas City, Missouri, made in 1847 a plan of the lands, dividing them into lots, and marking one lot, "Donated for graveyard." The plan was duly recorded, and the other lots were sold according to the plan.

---

[1] *Hagaman* v. *Dittmar*, 24 Kansas 42 (1880).

[2] *Hayes* v. *Hauke et al.*, 45 Kansas 466 (1891).

[3] *Commonwealth* v. *Viall*, 2 Allen (Mass.) 512 (1861).

Prior to the making of the plan, a very few burials had been made on a high knoll or ridge which lay near the northwestern corner of the square, extending the street on the north side, which was not distinguishable from the ground in controversy by any visible boundary at that time. Thenceforth the inhabitants of the town and vicinity continued to bury their dead in this land on the western half, which was its highest part, making use of the unimproved streets on the north and west for the same purpose.[1]

Where the owner of a certain lot of land stated to several people living in the vicinity that the ground might be used for a burial place, and he suffered it to be fenced and exclusively used for such a purpose for a great number of years, lots being appropriated, roads made in it (the expense being paid by subscription), etc., it is a sufficient dedication.[2]

Land may be dedicated to the use of only a limited portion of the public, and to a corporation as well as to a person.[3]

A special and express trust created by the appropriation of a lot of ground by a cemetery association, for the purpose of the exclusive burial of the dead of a certain church, will be upheld, and the execution of it strictly enforced in a court of equity, upon the application of any member of the church, where there has been an abuse or perversion of the trust.[4]

---

[1] *Campbell* v. *City of Kansas*, 102 Mo. 326 (1890).
[2] *Pierce* v. *Spafford*, 53 Vt. 394 (1881).
[3] *Mowry* v. *City of Providence*, 10 R. I. 52 (1871).
[4] *Hullman et al.* v. *Honcamp et al.*, 5 Ohio St. 237 (1855).

Nature of the Right parted with. — Dedication has respect to the possession and not to the permanent title, and the act is only one of estoppel.[1] The public takes an exclusive right for the purposes of a cemetery only, and such right continues until the place loses its identity as a burial ground.[2]

Time as an Ingredient of Dedication. — Lapse of time is not an essential ingredient, where the dedication can be established by acts on the part of the owner and the public, unequivocal in their character, though occurring on a single day. But when such evidence is lacking, long continued and uninterrupted use of land by the public, as for twenty years, with the knowledge and acquiescence of the owner, furnishes strong evidence of a dedication.[3]

Effect of Dedication. — All prior rights of parties to land except that of reversion, upon dedication of it to burial purposes, are waived and subornated to the public use for such purposes.[4]

After such dedication, the owner of the land has no right to remove the bodies, or to deface or pull down the gravestones or monuments erected to perpetuate their memory.[5]

Conveyance of the Right of the Public. — Where land has been dedicated to the public for cemetery uses, and has been used by the citizens in the vicin-

---

[1] *Boyce et al.* v. *Kalbaugh et al.*, 47 Md. 334 (1877); *Hunter* v. *Trustees of Sandy Hill*, 6 Hill (N. Y.) 407 (1844).

[2] *Hunter* v. *Trustees of Sandy Hill*, 6 Hill (N. Y.) 407 (1844).

[3] *Boyce et al.* v. *Kalbaugh et al.*, 47 Md. 334 (1877); *Hunter* v. *Trustees of Sandy Hill*, 6 Hill (N. Y.) 407 (1844); *Mowry* v. *City of Providence*, 10 R. I. 52 (1871).

[4] *Boyce et al.* v. *Kalbaugh et al.*, 47 Md. 334 (1877).

[5] *State* v. *Wilson*, 94 N. C. 1015 (1886).

ity of the premises, and they have cleared and fenced it, and for years subsequently buried their dead there, their incorporation years later gives no right to the corporation to petition for quietus of title against the widow of the original owner. The court held that the natural persons could not convey such a right, and that this was not the case of one suing in behalf of many.[1]

BY CONVEYANCE.

Land may be obtained for a cemetery by purchase, the title being passed by deed as in ordinary transfers of real estate. Where a deed of land sold to a cemetery association declares that the premises are conveyed for cemetery purposes, they must be so used, though a consideration was paid therefor.[2] However, if a deed is made of land "for a place of burial and for other purposes," it passes a title in fee simple, and there is no reversion.[3]

A grant of land to a church society for the use and purpose of a church and churchyard and a burying place is a grant for that special purpose, and when the purpose fails the land reverts to the original owner or his heirs. When such society dissolves and the church is abandoned, the burying ground may still be used as a place of burial by those who have relatives interred there.[4]

---

[1] *Redwood Cemetery Association* v. *Bandy et al.*, 93 Ind. 246 (1883).

[2] *Reed et al.* v. *Stouffer et al.*, 56 Md. 236 (1881).

[3] *M. P. Church of Cincinnati* v. *Laws et al.*, 7 Ohio C. C. 211 (1893).

[4] *Gumbert's Appeal*, 110 Pa. St. 496 (1885).

A deed to the trustees of a church is the same as if made to the church in its corporate name.[1]

BY RIGHT OF EMINENT DOMAIN.

The law of eminent domain is this, that private land may be taken for the public use,[2] a reasonable compensation being made therefor. When an application is made to a court for license to take and condemn land for cemeteries two questions arise: first, Is the purpose a public one? and, second, Is it necessary to take the land? The law is clear that a cemetery reasonably near a city or town is a necessity. The doubt arises when there are several cemeteries in the region already.

The Purpose of the Taking. — First, then, Is the cemetery for which the land is asked to be condemned and taken a private one, or is it for the use of the public? It is settled that land may be condemned for the purpose of establishing or enlarging a cemetery of a city or town, which is strictly the only public cemetery. The cemetery must be one in which the public in general have a right of interment.[3]

There are many cemeteries which are strictly private, in which the public have not, and cannot acquire, the right of interment. It is clear that land cannot be taken by right of eminent domain for

---

[1] *Brendle et al.* v. *German Reformed Congregation et al.*, 33 Pa. St 415 (1859).

[2] *F. R. B. Cemetery Association* v. *Redd*, 33 W. Va. 262 (1889).

[3] *Farneman et al.* v. *Mount Pleasant Cemetery Association*, 135 Ind. 344 (1893).

such cemeteries.[1] The doubt arises when the burial grounds of cemetery associations are considered. These are in a certain sense public, and in another sense private. The supreme court of Connecticut argues in favor of cemetery corporations, that "The safety of the living requires the burial of the dead in proper time and place; and inasmuch as it may so happen that no individual may be willing to sell land for such use, of necessity there must remain to the public the right to acquire and use it under such regulations as a proper respect for the memory of the dead and the feelings of survivors demands. In order to secure for burial places during a period extending indefinitely into the future that degree of care universally demanded, the legislature permits associations to exist with power to discharge in behalf and for the benefit of the public the duty of providing, maintaining, and protecting them. The use of land for this purpose does not cease to be a public use, because they require varying sums for rights to bury in different localities; not even if the cost of the right is in practical exclusion of some. Corporations take land by right of domain primarily for the benefit of the public, incidentally for the benefit of themselves; . . . it remains a public use as long as all persons have the same measure of right for the same measure of money."[2] The New York court differs from the court of Connecticut in its statement of the law. In the case of the *Deans-*

---

[1] *Evergreen Cemetery Association of New Haven* v. *Beecher et al.*, 53 Conn. 551 (1886).

[2] *Evergreen Cemetery Association* v. *City of New Haven*, 43 Conn. 234 (1875); *Evergreen Cemetery Association of New Haven* v. *Beecher et al.*, 53 Conn. 551 (1886).

ville Cemetery Association, the supreme court of New York [1] held that land taken by a private incorporated cemetery association was for a public use sufficient for this purpose, as provision for the proper and decent burial of the dead is a public necessity and duty. The court of appeals,[2] to which the case was carried, reversed the decision of the supreme court, and held that the "use of lands for the purposes of rural cemetery associations is private and not public. The right of the trustees is to divide the ground into lots, and sell them to individuals. There is no right on the part of the public to buy lots or bury their dead there. There is nothing in the cemetery in which the public, as such, have any interest. The fact that the burial of the dead is a public benefit, as some argue, does not make the cemetery public."

Statutes regarding the taking of land under this right of eminent domain must be strictly construed, as ownership and enjoyment of private property are almost sacred in the eye of the law, and the owner's right is subject only to that of the public. This great power is jealously guarded, and the use must be plainly a public one. It cannot be inferred that the use is public merely from the fact that a corporation asks for the land.[3]

The Necessity for the Taking. — The next question is whether the taking of land for cemetery purposes in each particular case is necessary. This need must be shown actually to exist, and not be simply

---

[1] *Deansville Cemetery Association*, 5 Hun (N. Y.) 482 (1875).
[2] *Deansville Cemetery Association*, 66 N. Y. 568 (1876).
[3] *F. R. B. Cemetery Association* v. *Redd*, 33 W. Va. 262 (1889).

a fanciful one.[1] The most difficult case to decide, as to the necessity of the taking of land for cemetery purposes, in those States where land is allowed to be taken for such uses under the right of eminent domain by other than cemeteries belonging to municipalities, is that of a religious organization which has outgrown its present limits and seeks to add to it or to open a new cemetery when extensive and beautiful public cemeteries have just been opened, to which all have a right. From a very early period in the history of the Christian church burying grounds were instituted and maintained by the church; and when the divisions in the faith and church took place the various denominations provided cemeteries for the interment of the people of their respective persuasions, and, with the exception of the Scotch Presbyterians and the New England Puritans, consecrated them with religious services. It is particularly true in New England, that in the early days the ecclesiastical society and the town were one; and when the towns grew, and of necessity a division into two or more parishes occurred, the same religious body that built the new meeting-house and settled the minister provided also the burying ground. They were all of them ecclesiastical burying places, though all in the parish probably had a right of interment therein. In the case of the *Application of St. Bernard & St. Lawrence Cemetery Association*,[2] the supreme court of Connecticut found that a

---

[1] *F. R. B. Cemetery Association* v. *Redd*, 33 W. Va. 262 (1889).

[2] *Application of St. Bernard & St. Lawrence Cemetery Association*, 58 Conn. 91 (1889).

Roman Catholic cemetery was of public necessity and convenience, the people of that faith constituting about one-third of the population of the town, and the only other Catholic cemetery in the town being full.

Who Decides these Questions? — Another question which arises under the subject of eminent domain is, Who is to decide whether the cemetery purposes are private or public, and whether the taking of the land is necessary? The supreme court [1] of New York, in the case of the *Deansville Cemetery Association*, held that the legislature, which provides for the taking of lands for cemetery purposes by cemetery associations by right of eminent domain, is the proper body to determine it; but the court of appeals,[2] to which the case was carried, held that it was a judicial question, and that the action of the legislature was not conclusive evidence that the use was a public one.

Application. — An application to court to take land for cemetery purposes under the right of eminent domain must show that the land is needed for public use, and that it will, when condemned and taken, be devoted to such use.[3]

Damages. — The cash market value of the land taken for cemetery purposes by the right of eminent domain, as found by a jury, must be paid to the owner.

---

[1] *Deansville Cemetery Association*, 5 Hun (N. Y.) 482 (1875).

[2] *Deansville Cemetery Association*, 66 N. Y. 568 (1876).

[3] *Evergreen Cemetery Association of New Haven* v. *Beecher et al.*, 53 Conn. 551 (1886); *F. R. B. Cemetery Association* v. *Redd*, 33 W. Va. 262 (1889).

REVERSION.

Where land has been dedicated to the use of the public as a burying ground, and the cemetery is subsequently legally abolished, the title to the land reverts to the original owner and his heirs and assigns; but not until then.[1] The public cannot use it for any other purpose under and by virtue of the dedication or the use made of it by the public.[2]

Where land is conveyed for a cemetery upon condition, the condition will be supported, and the land will revert upon breach thereof, although interments have been made therein. In the case of *Dolan et al. v. Mayor, &c. of City of Baltimore*,[3] a deed of a lot of land was made to the trustees of a certain church organization, in trust, to erect a Roman Catholic church and lay out a place on the same for the burial of the Roman Catholics of the city, and on the condition that if the trustees did not do this the lot should revert to the grantor and the deed be void. The trustees built the church elsewhere, but used the land exclusively for burial purposes. The court held that the condition was good and the deed void, and that the title to the land reverted to the grantor.

When a religious society which has received a conveyance of land for a churchyard, and has used it as such, dissolves, and the church has been aban-

---

[1] *Beatty et al. v. Trustees of German Lutheran Church of Georgetown*, 2 Peters (U. S.) 566 (1829).

[2] *Campbell v. City of Kansas*, 102 Mo. 326 (1890).

[3] *Dolan et al. v. Mayor, &c. of City of Baltimore*, 4 Gill (Md.) 394 (1846).

doned, the place may still be used as a burial ground by those who have relatives buried there, and the reversion will thus be prevented. Such parties have sufficient interest in the trust to clothe them with a right to preserve the cemetery. Hence, upon their petition, the court will set aside a sale of such property, made under an order of court, to an incorporated society, formed for the purpose of continuing the use of the ground as a burial place, especially when the interest of the parties who petitioned for such sale did not appear upon the record.[1]

American courts have very generally ignored or denied the existence of the doctrine of *cy pres* as bearing upon the donation and dedication of land for particular charitable uses, such as graveyards.[2]

When cemetery lands revert to the former owner, the relatives of those buried there have the right to remove the remains and monuments, and other fixtures that they and their ancestors have placed there.[2]

[1] *Gumbert's Appeal*, 110 Pa. St. 496 (1885).
[2] *Campbell* v. *City of Kansas*, 102 Mo. 326 (1890).

CHAPTER XVIII.

CEMETERIES AS NUISANCES.

A CEMETERY is not *per se* a nuisance.[1] It is necessary that the bodies of the dead be disposed of in some way; and burial in the earth, which is suggested by man's origin and destiny, is the common method. Their resting place is respected universally, and burying grounds are not only regarded as necessary, but are established, maintained, and stringently protected by law.[2] Not only are they not nuisances, but many modern cemeteries near cities are so located, and laid out with drives and walks, so ornamented with trees, shrubs, and flowers, and by monumental structures of elaborate design and statues and other exhibitions of sculpturesque skill, as to be beautiful and delightful even as a public park or landscape garden, being free from

---

[1] *Kingsbury* v. *Flowers*, 65 Ala. 479 (1880); *Town of Lake View* v. *Rose Hill Cemetery Co.*, 70 Ill. 191 (1873); *Begein et al.* v. *City of Anderson*, 28 Ind. 79 (1867); *Musgrove* v. *Catholic Church of St. Louis*, 10 La. Ann. 431 (1855); *City of New Orleans* v. *Wardens of the Church of St. Louis*, 11 La. Ann. 244 (1856); *Barnes* v. *Hathorn*, 54 Me. 124 (1866); *Monk* v. *Packard et al.*, 71 Me. 309 (1880); *Ellison* v. *Commissioners of Washington*, 5 Jones' Eq. (N. C.) 57 (1859); *Dunn* v. *City of Austin*, 77 Texas 139 (1890).

[2] *Begein et al.* v. *City of Anderson*, 28 Ind. 79 (1867); *Ellison* v. *Commissioners of Washington*, 5 Jones' Eq. (N. C.) 57 (1859).

every legitimate objection.[1] They attract and hold the attention of lovers of the beautiful in nature and art.

A properly conducted cemetery is not even disturbing to the senses of ordinary people. Persons of morbid or excitable imagination may shrink from the constant view of these fixed memorials of death and decay, which suggest so many unpleasant reflections, and be thereby mentally disquieted. Others are morally benefited by thoughts thus suggested. Superstitious fears may also exaggerate the importance of their presence. All sorts of horrible and ghoulish things may be imagined, and sickness follow as the result; but the human remains as they lie there properly interred cannot legally offend the senses. The stones alone are seen, and have the same effect that they would have if no remains lay beneath them.[2]

Cemeteries must not be far from cities and towns, and must generally be near private estates; and although they may depreciate their market value, they are not therefore legal nuisances.[3] Neither are unsightly or ill formed constructions nuisances because they offend the eye or taste; nor are vexatious and irritating acts.[4]

---

[1] *Town of Lake View* v. *Letz et al.*, 44 Ill. 81 (1867); *Town of Lake View* v. *Rose Hill Cemetery Co.*, 70 Ill. 191 (1873); *Monk* v. *Packard et al.*, 71 Me. 309 (1880).

[2] *Barnes* v. *Hathorn*, 54 Me. 124 (1866); *Monk* v. *Packard et al.*, 71 Me. 309 (1880); *Ellison* v. *Commissioners of Washington*, 5 Jones' Eq. (N. C.) 57 (1859).

[3] *City of New Orleans* v. *Wardens of the Church of St. Louis*, 11 La. Ann. 244 (1856); *Barnes* v. *Hathorn*, 54 Me. 124 (1866).

[4] *Barnes* v. *Hathorn*, 54 Me. 124 (1866).

At common law a man can bury his dead in his own land just as legally as he can sow seed or plant trees there; and what he can do himself he may permit others to do.[1] He has the right to improve and control his estate, and to make such erections as his judgment, taste, or interest may suggest, without the dictation or interference of his neighbors. But he must be reasonable in the use of his property; the health, comfort, and reasonable enjoyment of like rights of his neighbors must be deferred to.[2] The owner of every burial lot is bound to know at his peril that it may become offensive for various reasons, and, if it does, he must yield to laws for the suppression of nuisances.[3] There is nothing in nature that may not become mischievous; and one of the readiest instruments of harm is an improperly conducted cemetery.[4]

An important factor in the consideration of cemeteries as nuisances is the location of the burial ground. It may be situated in a place so remote from any settlement that what would be very obnoxious and decidedly harmful to health in other localities would be unobjectionable there. A burying ground within the limits of a city, where the population is dense, may readily become a nuisance.[5]

---

[1] *Application of St. Bernard & St. Lawrence Cemetery Association*, 58 Conn. 91 (1889).

[2] *Barnes* v. *Hathorn*, 54 Me. 124 (1866).

[3] *Brick Presbyterian Church* v. *Mayor, &c. of City of New York*, 5 Cowen (N. Y.) 538 (1826); *Went* v. *M. P. Church of Williamsburgh et al.*, 80 Hun (N. Y.) 266 (1894).

[4] *Town of Lake View* v. *Rose Hill Cemetery Co.*, 70 Ill. 191 (1873); *Dunn* v. *City of Austin*, 77 Texas 139 (1890).

[5] *Town of Lake View* v. *Letz et al.*, 44 Ill. 81 (1867); *Begein*

If the atmosphere is corrupted by bad odors emitted from the decaying bodies, either in tombs or graves, and health is or will be endangered thereby, the cemetery or tomb may be enjoined by a court of equity.[1] But it will not be prohibited for idle and unfounded fears of ill effects from the use thereof.[2] In the case of *Barnes* v. *Hathorn*,[2] a man in Maine built upon his land a tomb forty-four feet from the plaintiff's house. In the tomb, nine years before the time the action arose, nine bodies had been placed, and from them such an effluvia was emitted that the house of the plaintiff was rendered unwholesome. The bodies were removed upon the advice of a physician. A few days before this suit was brought, another body was deposited in the tomb, and, without waiting for any obnoxious results, the plaintiff at once petitioned the court for an injunction against the same, alleging that his life was uncomfortable, etc., by reason of his apprehension of danger therefrom. The majority of the court held that the apprehension of danger was well founded, and the prayer of the petition was granted. Justice Dickerson however dissented from the opinion of the majority, holding that in an unoccupied state the tomb could not have caused such substantial discomfort as the law imputes to a nuisance. The plaintiff's tastes may have been offended, and he might have been really apprehensive of danger, but

---

et al. v. *City of Anderson*, 28 Ind. 79 (1867); *Barnes* v. *Hathorn*, 54 Me. 124 (1866); *Dunn* v. *City of Austin*, 77 Texas 139 (1890).

[1] *Monk* v. *Packard et al.*, 71 Me. 309 (1880); *Clark* v. *Lawrence, tr.*, 6 Jones' Eq. (N. C.) 83 (1860).

[2] *Barnes* v. *Hathorn*, 54 Me. 124 (1866).

the fact that the body remained in the tomb only from October to December does not constitute it a nuisance, no offensive vapor having arisen therefrom. There was no evidence to indicate that the deposit was otherwise than temporary, — for the winter only. The justice said that this position of the court would make every receiving tomb a nuisance, as they are built out of the ground, etc.

A cemetery may be a nuisance because it contaminates wells and springs of water. If it does, equity will grant relief by injunction.[1] But the establishment of a cemetery which may result in the pollution of subterranean streams of water is not a nuisance, and cannot be enjoined.[2] The law does not protect fancies merely, but will prevent real wrong and injury combined.[3]

A cemetery becomes a public nuisance when it affects the public generally, and a private nuisance when individuals only are affected. If an individual sustains special damage to himself beyond that which is common to the public by reason of a public nuisance, he may maintain an action for such special injury.[4]

When a cemetery or tomb becomes a private nuisance, if it is on the highway it is a public nuisance also, as every traveller on that way suffers the effects of it.[5]

In these cases the plaintiff, if he would succeed

---

[1] *Clark* v. *Lawrence, tr.*, 6 Jones' Eq. (N. C.) 83 (1860).
[2] *City of Greencastle* v. *Hazelett*, 23 Ind. 186 (1864).
[3] *Monk* v. *Packard et al.*, 71 Me. 309 (1880).
[4] *Barnes* v. *Hathorn*, 54 Me. 124 (1866).
[5] *Monk* v. *Packard et al.*, 71 Me. 309 (1880).

in enjoining a cemetery, must not be himself a contributor to his discomfort and to the injury to his health. He ought not to build a dwelling-house by the cemetery, and then ask the court to enjoin it.[1]

Practice. — Where a private burying ground is owned by two persons, they should be joined as respondents in a bill for an injunction against further interments therein; and if one of them dies before the bill is filed, the widow of the deceased, having a right of sepulture therein, her second husband, and the heirs, should be joined with the survivor, but not the personal representative.[2]

In such a bill facts should be stated, and not the general allegation that injury to the health of the family of the complainant, or other injurious consequences, will probably be caused by the pollution of the air and water.[2]

---

[1] *Ellison* v. *Commissioners of Washington*, 5 Jones' Eq. (N. C.) 57 (1859).

[2] *Kingsbury* v. *Flowers*, 65 Ala. 479 (1880).

CHAPTER XIX.

CEMETERIES AS CHARITIES.

A CEMETERY corporation is not a public charity at common law, although it voluntarily uses its funds for objects akin to the purposes of its organization.[1] Neither are the lots,[2] graves,[3] tombs,[4] vaults,[5] gravestones,[6] nor monuments[7] in cemeteries charitable

[1] *Donnelly* v. *Boston Catholic Cemetery Association*, 146 Mass. 163 (1888).

[2] *Bates, adm'r,* v. *Bates,* 134 Mass. 110 (1883); *Bartlett et al., ex'rs et tr's, petitioners,* 163 Mass. 509 (1895); *Moore's ex'r* v. *Moore et al.,* 50 N. J. Eq. 554 (1892).

[3] *Fowler* v. *Fowler,* 33 Beav. (Eng.) 616 (1864); *Fiske* v. *Attorney General,* L. R. 4 Eq. (Eng.) 521 (1867); *In re Birkett,* L. R. 9 Ch. Div. (Eng.) 576 (1878); *Detwiller* v. *Hartman,* 37 N. J. Eq. 349 (1883); *Hartson, ex'r,* v. *Elden et al.,* 50 N. J. Eq. 522 (1892); *Moore's ex'r* v. *Moore et al.,* 50 N. J. Eq. 554 (1892).

[4] *Doe* v. *Pitcher et al.,* 6 Taun. (Eng.) 359 (1815); *Lloyd* v. *Lloyd,* 2 Simons' Ch., N. S. (Eng.) 255 (1852); *Rickard* v. *Robson,* 31 Beav. (Eng.) 244 (1862); *In re Williams,* L. R. 5 Ch. Div. (Eng.) 735 (1877); *Bates, adm'r,* v. *Bates,* 134 Mass. 110 (1883).

[5] *Doe* v. *Pitcher et al.,* 6 Taun. (Eng.) 359 (1815); *Hoare* v. *Osborne,* L. R. 1 Eq. (Eng.) 585 (1866); *Vaughn* v. *Thomas,* L. R. 33 Ch. Div. (Eng.) 187 (1886).

[6] *Hunter* v. *Bullock,* L. R. 14 Eq. (Eng.) 45 (1872); *Dawson* v. *Small,* L. R. 18 Eq. (Eng.) 114 (1874); *In re Birkett,* L. R. 9 Ch. Div. (Eng.) 576 (1878).

[7] *Hoare* v. *Osborne,* L. R. 1 Eq. (Eng.) 585 (1866); *Bartlett et al., ex'rs et tr's, petitioners,* 163 Mass. 509 (1895); *Detwiller* v. *Hartman,* 37 N. J. Eq. 349 (1883); *Hartson, ex'r,* v. *Elden et al.,* 50 N. J. Eq. 522 (1892).

objects. And as none of these are public charities no fund can be established *in perpetuam* to care for or repair and maintain them. Such funds and attempts to form them are void.[1] In the case of *Doe* v. *Pitcher et al.*,[2] land was granted in trust to repair a vault and tomb standing on the land perpetually, to rebuild them, if necessary, and to permit them to be used as family vaults for the donor and his family, and the court held that the grant was void as it would otherwise create a perpetuity. In the case of *Rickard* v. *Robson*,[3] the interest of the fund was to be applied to keeping up the tombs of the testator and his family; and, in *Fowler* v. *Fowler*,[4] to the maintenance of the testator's family graves. The case of *Hoare* v. *Osborne*[5] was one where six hundred pounds was bequeathed to trustees, the income to be paid to the minister and church wardens of the parish, to be applied by them

---

[1] *Doe* v. *Pitcher et al.*, 6 Taun. (Eng.) 359 (1815); *Lloyd* v. *Lloyd*, 2 Simons' Ch., N. S. (Eng.) 255 (1852); *Rickard* v. *Robson*, 31 Beav. (Eng.) 244 (1862); *Fowler* v. *Fowler*, 33 Beav. (Eng.) 616 (1864); *Hoare* v. *Osborne*, L. R. 1 Eq. (Eng.) 585 (1866); *Fiske* v. *Attorney General*, L. R. 4 Eq. (Eng.) 521 (1867); *Hunter* v. *Bullock*, L. R. 14 Eq. (Eng.) 45 (1872); *Dawson* v. *Small*, L. R. 18 Eq. (Eng.) 114 (1874); *In re Williams*, L. R. 5 Ch. Div. (Eng.) 735 (1877); *In re Birkett*, L. R. 9 Ch. Div. (Eng.) 576 (1878); *Bates, adm'r*, v. *Bates*, 134 Mass. 110 (1883); *Bartlett et al., ex'rs et tr's, petitioners*, 163 Mass. 509 (1895); *Detwiller* v. *Hartman*, 37 N. J. Eq. 349 (1883); *Hartson, ex'r*, v. *Elden et al.*, 50 N. J. Eq. 522 (1892); *Moore's ex'r* v. *Moore et al.*, 50 N. J. Eq. 554 (1892).

[2] *Doe* v. *Pitcher et al.*, 6 Taun. (Eng.) 359 (1815).
[3] *Rickard* v. *Robson*, 31 Beav. (Eng.) 244 (1862).
[4] *Fowler* v. *Fowler*, 33 Beav. (Eng.) 616 (1864).
[5] *Hoare* v. *Osborne*, L. R. 1 Eq. (Eng.) 585 (1866).

to keeping in "good repair, order, and condition" forever the monument of the testatrix' mother in the church, the vault in the churchyard in which she was interred, and an ornamental window which the testatrix directed her trustees to place in the church in memory of her mother, etc. The gift for the repair of the vault was held invalid, it being in the churchyard; but the rest was held good, on the ground that as they were within the church they were repairs of the same, and therefore valid. In the case of *Dawson* v. *Small*,[1] six hundred pounds were placed in trust to be invested and the income applied to keeping in good repair all the tombstones and headstones of the testator's relatives and himself in a certain churchyard, in which he was to be buried.

The objection to these bequests, as has already been said, lies in their creation of funds that are to continue without limitation. And the same objection arises when a testator gives his executor permissive power to use certain funds for such purposes.[2]

The gift or appropriation of money by a testator for the erection of a monument, etc., does not come under that ban, and is valid.[3] In the case of *Gilmer's legatees* v. *Gilmer's ex'rs*,[3] a bequest for the erection of monuments to the memory "of Gen. Stonewall Jackson, of Virginia, and Col's. Thomas Cobb and Barstow, of Georgia," was held to be good; and, in the same case, another bequest "for assisting to raise monuments to the memory of all

---

[1] *Dawson* v. *Small*, L. R. 18 Eq. (Eng.) 114 (1874).
[2] *Hartson, ex'r,* v. *Elden et al.*, 50 N. J. Eq. 522 (1892).
[3] *Gilmer's legatees* v. *Gilmer's ex'rs*, 42 Ala. 9 (1868).

other officers and soldiers from the State of Alabama who distinguished themselves, or those who have died from wounds or were killed in defence of their country, in the present war between the United States and Confederate States," was held to be void on account of the impossibility of its performance.

A gift may be made, however, to a charity on condition that it should keep a tomb in repair, etc., and thus the desired purpose can be accomplished.[1]

[1] *Tyler* v. *Tyler*, L. R., 1891, 3 Ch. Div. (Eng.) 252 (1890).

CHAPTER XX.

RULES AND REGULATIONS.

Of the validity of rules and regulations of cemeteries and matters connected therewith, their reasonableness is the test.

Municipal By-Laws and Ordinances. — A by-law of a city or town, in order to be valid, must be reasonable.[1] By-laws which require dead bodies to be buried below a certain depth, or to be buried away from a place densely populated, or liable to become so, or within a reasonable time after death, etc., are all reasonable and valid, as otherwise a nuisance might be created.[2] But it is doubtful if the interment of the dead can be taken out of the hands of the relatives if they are able and willing to attend to it, and the validity of a by-law to that designed effect is equally uncertain.[3] In the case of *Ritchey* v. *City of Canton*,[4] a person bought of a cemetery corporation a lot in its cemetery,

---

[1] *Bogert* v. *City of Indianapolis*, 13 Ind. 134 (1859); *Austin et al.* v. *Murray*, 16 Pick. (Mass.) 121 (1834); *Commonwealth* v. *Goodrich*, 13 Allen (Mass.) 546 (1866); *City of Austin* v. *Austin City Cemetery Association*, 87 Texas, 330 (1894).

[2] *Ritchey* v. *City of Canton*, 46 Ill. App. 185 (1891); *Bogert* v. *City of Indianapolis*, 13 Ind. 134 (1859).

[3] *Bogert* v. *City of Indianapolis*, 13 Ind. 134 (1859).

[4] *Ritchey* v. *City of Canton*, 46 Ill. App. 185 (1891).

and subsequently the company transferred its cemetery property to the city in which it was situated. Afterward the city council passed an ordinance providing that no grave should be dug in the cemetery except by permission, and under the direction of the city sexton. It was held that the owner of the lot could not by such an ordinance be deprived of the right to dig a grave or have one dug in his lot in a safe and proper manner. In the case of *Commonwealth* v. *Goodrich*,[1] a regulation of a city, that no person, other than superintendents of cemeteries or duly licensed undertakers " shall dig any grave, bury any dead body, or open any tomb in any cemetery, graveyard, or other place in the city other than the cemetery, or move from any house or place within the city to any place of burial whatsoever, the body of any deceased person," was held to be reasonable and valid, as only suitable persons — those that are trustworthy and possessed of requisite knowledge and skill — should be allowed to transport dead bodies through the streets of a city, and inter the same, and as the public health of the city depends to a great degree upon the sanitary methods in such cases. In the case of *Austin et al.* v. *Murray*,[2] it was held that a by-law of a town, which prohibits all persons, without license from the selectmen, from burying any dead body brought into the town on any part of their own premises, or elsewhere within the town, was reasonable if the town was large and densely populated, or if the by-law limited the prohibition in its application to the populous portion of the town;

[1] *Commonwealth* v. *Goodrich*, 13 Allen (Mass.) 546 (1866).
[2] *Austin et al.* v. *Murray*, 16 Pick. (Mass.) 121 (1834).

but that it would be unreasonable, and therefore invalid, being an unnecessary restraint upon the right of interment, if it applied to a country town in all its territory.

A city cannot interfere in any way, by by-laws or otherwise, with cemeteries beyond the city limits, which the city has not established, and does not own or control.[1]

By-Laws of Cemetery Associations. — Rules and regulations of cemetery corporations governing lot owners must be general in their application, and equally affect all the owners, and be reasonable, in order to be valid.[2] And a lot owner's rights cannot be abridged by the passage of unreasonable by-laws subsequently to his purchase of the lot.[3]

Denominational Cemeteries. — Churches may establish rules for the government of cemeteries belonging to them, but cannot restrict or affect the police power of the State, nor determine questions affecting property rights or other secular matters. The only other test of their validity is their reasonableness. They must become operative and be made known to the owner of a lot before he purchases it of the church.[4]

---

[1] *Begein et al. v. City of Anderson*, 28 Ind. 79 (1867).

[2] *Rosehill Cemetery Co. v. Hopkinson, ex'x*, 114 Ill. 209 (1885).

[3] *Mt. Moriah Cemetery Association v. Commonwealth*, 81 Pa. St. 235 (1876).

[4] *Dwenger et al. v. Geary et al.*, 113 Ind. 106 (1887).

CHAPTER XXI.

TAXATION.

At common law, cemeteries and the property within them were taxable as other property was, and could be sold on execution for taxes as other property unless exempted by its charter.[1] The graves, however, would not be allowed to be desecrated.[2] But now all cemeteries are exempt from general taxation by force of statutes in the several States of the Union. They are thus exempted in two ways, first, by a general statute, and, second, by a clause in the charter when they are specially incorporated.

The reason of this exemption is not the financial benefit to cemetery associations, but the preservation of burial places for the use to which they are appropriated, and to secure their perpetuity as resting places of the dead, and thus guard against their desecration, which would result if the property were liable to be sold for taxes,[3] and, if it were sold to be kept as it is, filled with graves perhaps, it could not be of any value to the purchaser, and the law will not allow it to be

---

[1] *Bloomington Cemetery Association* v. *People*, 139 Ill. 16 (1891).

[2] *Louisville* v. *Nevins, &c.*, 10 Bush (Ky.) 549 (1874).

[3] *Proprietors of Cemetery of Mount Auburn* v. *Mayor, &c. of Cambridge et al.*, 150 Mass. 12 (1889).

desecrated.[1] The court will construe the statute in the broad sense, having this end in view.[2]

What is meant by Taxes. — The New Jersey court says that the words "taxation" and "assessments," as used in the statutes exempting cemetery property from taxation, are not of the same import; the first referring to the raising of revenue, and being general; the second relating to improvements, and being special.[3] The Maryland court holds, however, that the words mean the same thing.[4] In the case of *City of Baltimore* v. *Proprietors of Green Mount Cemetery*,[4] the cemetery by its charter was not "liable to any tax or public imposition whatever," and the court held that the exemption included any tax for revenue, and did not include expense of opening a street, "and such charges as are inseparably incident to its location in regard to other property."

Where cemeteries are exempted from "all public taxes," sewer assessments are public taxes, and therefore exempt.[5] In the case of *Olive Cemetery Co.* v. *City of Philadelphia*,[6] the charter of a cemetery corporation exempted it from taxation except for State purposes; and the court held that the lots were not taxable for a sewer in the street next them.

Where the exemption is from "all public taxes and

[1] *State, &c.* v. *City of St. Paul*, 36 Minn. 529 (1887).

[2] *Louisville* v. *Nevin, &c.*, 10 Bush (Ky.) 549 (1874).

[3] *Protestant Foster Home* v. *Mayor, &c. of City of Newark*, 36 N. J. L. 478 (1873).

[4] *City of Baltimore* v. *Proprietors of Green Mount Cemetery*, 7 Md. 517 (1855).

[5] *State, &c.* v. *City of St. Paul*, 36 Minn. 529 (1887).

[6] *Olive Cemetery Co.* v. *City of Philadelphia*, 93 Pa. St. 129 (1880).

assessments," building a sidewalk in front of the cemetery is an expense for which the cemetery is not liable to be assessed.[1]

If cemeteries are exempted from general taxation only, they can be taxed for local improvements, as for building and repairing streets.[2]

Where lands of a cemetery corporation are, by its charter, exempt from "taxation of any kind," it embraces the land, with the permanent improvements thereon, but not a fund invested in stocks the interest of which is devoted to the maintenance of the cemetery, the land and the fixtures thereon which it owns being exempt, but not its personal property.[3]

Kind of Property Exempted. — Permanent improvements on the cemetery lands, which are essential to its use and enjoyment as a burial ground, are treated the same as the lands themselves; if one is exempt, the other is.[4]

What Land is Exempted. — A large lot of land bought for burial purposes is exempt from taxation under the statute, although there are only two graves in it;[5] but land belonging to a cemetery corporation

---

[1] *State, &c.* v. *City of St. Paul*, 36 Minn. 529 (1887).

[2] *Bloomington Cemetery Association* v. *People*, 139 Ill. 16 (1891); *Buffalo City Cemetery* v. *City of Buffalo*, 46 N. Y. 506 (1871); *Buffalo City Cemetery* v. *City of Buffalo*, 43 Hun (N. Y.) 127 (1887); *Buffalo City Cemetery* v. *City of Buffalo*, 118 N. Y. 61 (1889); *Lima* v. *Lima Cemetery Association*, 42 Ohio St. 128 (1884); *City of New Castle* v. *Stone Church Graveyard*, 33 Atl. Rep. (Pa.) 236 (1895).

[3] *State* v. *Wilson, &c.*, 52 Md. 638 (1879).

[4] *Appeal Tax Court* v. *Baltimore Cemetery Co.*, 50 Md. 432 (1878); *State* v. *Wilson, &c.*, 52 Md. 638 (1879).

[5] *Appeal Tax Court* v. *Zion Church of Baltimore*, 50 Md. 321 (1878).

not actually in use for burial purposes may be sold for a special tax like that of a private owner, unless exempted by its charter.[1] In the case of *Mulroy* v. *Churchman et al.*,[2] a lot of forty acres was held as a cemetery, but only one acre was in actual use for burial purposes, it being partially fenced off from the rest, which was used as farm land, the court held that the balance of the lot was taxable. The case of *Appeal Tax Court* v. *Zion Church of Baltimore*[3] was that of a churchyard from which all bodies but two had been removed. The two that remained were those of former pastors of the church, and had been buried there more than forty years. The then incumbent of the church was also expected to be buried there. The court held that no part of the lot was taxable.

The New Jersey court holds that the rule is that, if the amount of land owned by the cemetery company, although not all buried over, is proper in amount, — that is, that there is no more of it than will be probably required within a few years, — it is all exempt from taxation.[4]

Where a cemetery association was incorporated under a special act which provided that it might purchase a certain tract of land for cemetery purposes, that "said corporation [shall not] be liable to be

---

[1] *Bloomington Cemetery Association* v. *People*, 139 Ill. 16 (1891). This was the case of an unoccupied portion of a cemetery.

[2] *Mulroy* v. *Churchman et al.*, 52 Iowa 238 (1879).

[3] *Appeal Tax Court* v. *Zion Church of Baltimore*, 50 Md. 321 (1878).

[4] *City of Hoboken* v. *Inhabitants of North Bergen*, 43 N. J. L. 146 (1881).

taxed for said land," that it might erect a dwelling-house, etc., and set off a garden; and fifteen years later the corporation purchased a lot of land on the opposite side of the highway from the cemetery, and laid it out into burial lots and avenues, having upon it a small dwelling-house occupied by the superintendent of the cemetery, who paid no rent therefor, the use being a part of his salary, and two small barns used for the keeping of the horse, carts, and tools owned by the corporation for the work in the cemetery; and three years subsequently the corporation was authorized by statute to take and hold, by purchase or otherwise, so much real or personal estate as was necessary to its objects, and to be used for such objects; it was held that the new lot was thereby rendered exempt from taxation, it not being necessary to have that effect that the new lot should adjoin the original lot.[1]

A charter of a cemetery corporation which exempts its property from taxation "so long as the same shall remain dedicated to the purpose of a cemetery," cannot be made to include a lot of land on the opposite side of the road from the cemetery, which is rented to the sexton, who uses it as a residence and for the purposes of husbandry, and who pays rent therefor.[2] In the case of *People* v. *Graceland Cemetery Co.*,[3] a lot of land owned by the cemetery company was situated across the street from the cemetery, and the

---

[1] *Proprietors of Rural Cemetery* v. *County Commissioners of Worcester*, 152 Mass. 408 (1890).

[2] *Evangelical Lutheran Cemetery Association* v. *Lange, assessor*, 16 Mo. App. 468 (1885).

[3] *People* v. *Graceland Cemetery Co.*, 86 Ill. 336 (1877).

court held, though it was platted and recorded as cemetery lands, but never used as such, and the company had erected thereon a stable and some houses, occupied by men in the employ of the company, and removed mould and sand therefrom, and used it as needed in repairing the ground actually used for cemetery purposes, that such use of the property did not render it exempt from taxation under the terms and spirit of the charter, which exempted from taxation all property held and actually used by the corporation for burial purposes, or for the general uses of lot holders, or subservient to burial uses, and which had been platted and recorded as cemetery grounds.

Who should be Assessed. — As the corporation is the owner in fee of the land of an incorporated cemetery association, purchased for the purposes of the association, it is proper to assess the tax, when it is assessable against any one, for the whole premises upon the corporation, and not upon the lots to their individual owners.[1]

Effect of Prohibition of Interments. — Where lands are thus exempt from taxation under a statute, they will remain exempt, though no dead body is buried therein, when burials therein are prohibited by a valid city ordinance passed after the lands were acquired.[2]

Collection of Taxes. — Where cemetery lands are allowed to be assessed for taxes, the law will not

---

[1] *Buffalo City Cemetery* v. *City of Buffalo*, 46 N. Y. 503 (1871).

[2] *Oak Hill Cemetery Association* v. *Pratt et al., assessors*, 129 N. Y. 68 (1891).

permit the cemetery as such to be disturbed. The collection must be enforced in equity.[1]

Quashing Assessments, etc. — To quash the proceedings of the mayor and aldermen, and restrain the collector of the city from selling cemetery lands for taxes, procedure is by writ of *certiorari*.[2]

---

[1] *Lima v. Lima Cemetery Association*, 42 Ohio St. 128 (1884).

[2] *Proprietors of Cemetery of Mount Auburn v. Mayor, &c. of Cambridge et al.*, 150 Mass. 12 (1889); *Proprietors of Rural Cemetery v. County Commissioners of Worcester*, 152 Mass. 408 (1890).

CHAPTER XXII.

SALE, MORTGAGE, AND PARTITION OF CEMETERY PROPERTY.

The law regarding the sale, mortgage, and partition of cemetery property is necessarily different from that relating to other kinds of real estate.

SALE OF CEMETERY PROPERTY.

Good order, decency, and a just regard for the dead require that a lot used for the burial of the dead, while such use is existing, shall not be sold. Where a man bought a lot in a cemetery for the burial of himself and his family, and his wife greatly improved the lot at her and her husband's expense, and her parents and one of her sons and a brother of the husband had been buried therein, if her husband sells the lot for a valuable consideration to a stranger, the wife can maintain an action restraining the husband from conveying it. She is also entitled to have judgment entered therein, specifically devoting the lot to the objects for which it had been purchased and improved.[1]

Sale on Execution. — Burial lots are generally exempt by statute from levy and sale on execution.

---

[1] *Schroder* v. *Wanzor*, 36 Hun (N. Y.) 423 (1885).

MORTGAGE OF CEMETERY PROPERTY.

All cemeteries other than private ones are public in their nature, says the Minnesota court, and cannot be mortgaged.[1] The Pennsylvania court, however, holds that they can be;[2] and so, as in the case of eminent domain, the question whether a large proportion of our cemeteries are public or private in their nature is far from settled.

The mortgagee of a burial ground takes the mortgage with notice of the purposes to which the ground is devoted, and he is bound by the rights of burial, temporary or perpetual, granted by the mortgagor while in possession;[3] and he cannot desecrate the cemetery.[4]

Where a cemetery association made a mortgage of their cemetery grounds, a stone curbing which they had placed around a burial lot still owned by the association, and a monument which they had erected on the lot, consisting of a stone foundation extending below the frost line, and having upon the foundation a marble base surmounted by a marble shaft, and upon the shaft a statue, the whole being cemented together, and the entire work being built for the ornamentation of the grounds, the curbing and monument are so fixed to the realty as to be a part thereof, and

---

[1] *Wolford v. Crystal Lake Cemetery Association*, 54 Minn. 440 (1893).

[2] *Oakland Cemetery Co. v. Bancroft*, 161 Pa. St. 197 (1894).

[3] *Moreland et al. v. Richardson et al.*, 24 Beav. (Eng.) 33 (1857).

[4] *Moreland et al. v. Richardson et al.*, 22 Beav. (Eng.) 596 (1856).

to pass with the realty under the mortgage. They are not personal property, nor trade fixtures, and were intended to be a part of the realty.[1] Of course, such things in a lot of a person having only the easement of burial would be personal property.

In the case of *Lautz* v. *Buckingham*,[2] the court held that the mortgage of a lot in a cemetery given back to the owner of the cemetery at the time of the purchase thereof is good, and can be enforced ; and that the statute which exempts burial lots from sale on execution does not apply to voluntary acts of the owner.

PARTITION OF CEMETERY PROPERTY.

When a church owns a cemetery, and a division of the church takes place, the cemetery ought not to be divided also.[3]

---

[1] *Oakland Cemetery Co.* v. *Bancroft*, 161 Pa. St. 197 (1894).
[2] *Lautz* v. *Buckingham*, 4 Lans. (N. Y.) 484 (1871).
[3] *Brown* v. *Lutheran Church*, 23 Pa. St. 495 (1854).

CHAPTER XXIII.

CARE AND CONDUCT OF CEMETERIES.

The general control of cemeteries is under those parties who have the freehold in general possession. Cities can control only such cemeteries as belong to them;[1] and cemetery associations, etc., are limited to the control of their own cemeteries. After the dedication of land to burial uses of the people of the neighborhood, the original owner has no greater control of it than the neighbors, of whom he is one, who bury their dead there.[2]

The general owners of the freehold must adopt measures for the security of the grounds, establish avenues, and refrain from injuring private property of lot owners that is rightfully in the cemeteries.[3]

Lots sold to individuals are to be cared for by the owners, and not by the association;[4] even though

---

[1] *Wood et al.* v. *Macon and Brunswick R. R. Co. et al.*, 68 Ga. 539 (1882); *Bogert* v. *City of Indianapolis*, 13 Ind. 134 (1859).

[2] *Pierce* v. *Spafford*, 53 Vt. 394 (1881).

[3] *Wood et al.* v. *Macon and Brunswick R. R. Co. et al.*, 68 Ga. 539 (1882).

[4] *Bourland et al.* v. *Springdale Cemetery Association*, 56 Ill. App. 298 (1894); *Bourland* v. *Springdale Cemetery Association*, 42 N. E. Rep. (Ill.) 86 (1895).

the charter provides that the association out of the proceeds of sales of lots shall "keep the grounds in repair and in good order." [1]

The Puritan founders of New England chose the most bleak and barren spots for their burial places, and kept them so, as Whittier truly says: —

> "Our vales are sweet with fern and rose,
>   Our hills are maple-crowned;
> But not from them our fathers chose
>   The village burying ground.
>
> "The dreariest spot in all the land
>   To Death they set apart;
> With scanty grace from Nature's hand,
>   And none from that of Art.
>
> . . . .
>
> "For thus our fathers testified —
>   That he might read who ran —
> The emptiness of human pride,
>   The nothingness of man."

But since those early days the sentiment of the community has entirely changed, and refinements introduced by modern taste have commended themselves to general approbation. Public authorities as well as cemetery associations now skilfully embellish their various cemeteries with trees and shrubs and flowers, and works of art.[2] Beautiful creations of taste and genius relieve the external gloom, and soften the

---

[1] *Bourland v. Springdale Cemetery Association et al.*, 158 Ill. 458 (1895).

[2] *Wood et al. v. Macon and Brunswick R. R. Co. et al.*, 68 Ga. 539 (1882); *Town of Lake View v. Rose Hill Cemetery Co.*, 70 Ill. 191 (1873).

repulsive associations of the grave. Skill and taste should be applied to the grading, arrangement of avenues, alleys, and squares, and in the planting of trees and shrubbery.[1]

In order to insure regularity, permanence, and progress, it is absolutely necessary that there should be a general power of control in some one body, acting in pursuance of a matured and harmonious design.[1] Lot owners must not have control of the grounds beyond their lots, and even in them they are limited to acts of preservation and embellishment, restricted in some degree by the general opinion of the community.[2]

If the officers of a corporation fail to keep the walks, drives, and approaches of its cemetery in proper repair, a lot owner can maintain a bill in equity against them.[3]

In the case of *Perkins* v. *City of Lawrence*,[4] in a cemetery belonging to the city the authorities built a wall and terrace in a vacant triangular space, and closed the avenue which ran by it, but did not impair the means of access to or value of the lot of the plaintiff which he had purchased before the wall and terrace were built. The court found that the alteration was made in good faith for the improvement of the cemetery, and held that the owner of the lot, not being injured, could not object.

---

[1] *Seymour* v. *Page*, 33 Conn. 61 (1865).

[2] *Seymour* v. *Page*, 33 Conn. 61 (1865); *Commonwealth* v. *Viall*, 2 Allen (Mass.) 512 (1861).

[3] *Houston Cemetery Co. et al.* v. *Drew et al.*, 36 S. W. Rep. (Texas) 802 (1896).

[4] *Perkins* v. *City of Lawrence*, 138 Mass. 361 (1885).

Where towns are authorized by the legislature " to provide burial grounds," and no further directions are given, they are not limited as to the amount of money to be raised therefor, the quantity of land to be appropriated for the purpose, nor how it shall be fenced, laid out, arranged, or managed, and they are not prohibited from making it beautiful and attractive, instead of unsightly and repulsive; the exercise of their judgment extending to matters of taste in respect to both.[1] In the case of *Commonwealth* v. *Viall*,[2] which was one concerning the cutting of trees by the owner of the soil, who had dedicated the burial ground to the use of the people of the neighborhood years before, and it had been extensively used by them for interments, and before the trees were cut had been taken by the town as a public cemetery, Justice Hoar said : " The growth of these trees may have been watched with affectionate interest by friends and relatives of the departed, whose last resting place has been made more pleasant to the imagination of the survivors by the thought that it might become a resort of birds, and a place for wild flowers to grow; that waving boughs would shelter it from summer heat and protect it from the bleak winds of the ocean. The fallen leaf and withered branch are emblems of mortality; and in the opinion of many a tree is a more natural and fitting decoration of a cemetery than a costly monument."

A cemetery is protected by law in respect to the ornamental portion of it, as well as the more matter-

---

[1] *Jenkins et al.* v. *Inhabitants of Andover et al.*, 103 Mass. 94 (1869).

[2] *Commonwealth* v. *Viall*, 2 Allen (Mass.) 512 (1861).

of-fact and substantial and necessary parts.[1] Statutes have been passed in most of the States, if not all, to this effect. Even the birds that hibernate there are thus protected in some States.

[1] *Evergreen Cemetery Association* v. *City of New Haven*, 43 Conn. 234 (1875).

CHAPTER XXIV.

RIGHTS AND LIABILITIES OF LOT OWNERS.

The tenure of a lot owner depends not only upon the terms of the deed itself, but upon the act of incorporation of the cemetery from which the title is derived, and to the limitations of its powers, and the manifest intent of the parties to the instrument.

The burial of dead bodies in the land of a third person without right, and without the consent of the owner, gives no title thereto or interest therein, until a prescriptive or other right or title can be shown.[1]

Tenure. — Every owner of a burial lot must be deemed to have purchased and to hold it for the sole purpose of using it as a place of burial.[2]

A deed of a burial lot from a cemetery association, if they have power to make such a conveyance, the habendum clause being "to have and to hold," etc., to the said, etc., "his heirs and assigns, for the uses of sepulture only, and to or for no other whatever, subject, however, to the condition and limitation and with the privileges specified in the rules and regulations now made or that may hereafter be made and adopted

---

[1] *Bonham* v. *Loeb*, 18 So. Rep. (Ala.) 300 (1895).
[2] *Went* v. *M. P. Church of Williamsburgh et al.*, 80 Hun (N. Y.) 266 (1894).

by the managers of the said cemetery for the government of the lot holders and visitors of the same," passes the fee and the possession, though the company is to have the general care and management of the cemetery, it not being incompatible with the rights of the lot owners to manage their own lots.[1]

Generally, the right in the lot is an easement only, the right to use it for burial and cemetery purposes, but with no other interest in the fee.[2] But under the peculiar nature of the subject matter, as an easement cannot be gained except by deed or by a prescription of long standing, the courts term the right of burial in lots a license only, though with one or two exceptions they have all the qualities of easements. In the case of *Conger* v. *Treadway*,[3] a conveyance of land having been made to ten persons, on condition that the same was conveyed "for the purpose of a cemetery or burying place for the dead, and for no other purpose," a man bought a lot therein, but did not obtain a deed, which was promised to him, and he buried his dead in the lot from time to time, and erected monuments and beautified the lot, to the knowledge of the owner, the court held that the title to the land itself did not pass, but the exclusive right of burial did, no formal deed being necessary. A certificate of a burial lot, signed by the secretary of the board of trustees of a cemetery association only, without seal or other formality, passes no interest in the land, as an easement

---

[1] *N. Y. Bay Cemetery Co.* v. *Buckmaster*, 49 N. J. L. 449 (1887).

[2] *Buffalo City Cemetery* v. *City of Buffalo*, 46 N. Y. 503 (1871).

[3] *Conger* v. *Treadway*, 50 Hun (N. Y.) 451 (1888).

or otherwise; it is a license only.[1] The following is a copy of the certificate in the case of *McGuire, adm'r, v. Trustees of St. Patrick's Cathedral*,[2] which was held to convey a license only: —

"No. 726. Calvary Cemetery,
"266 Mulberry Street. New York, Nov. 22, 1870.
"Received from John McGuire ten dollars, being the amount of purchase money of a grave two feet by eight in Calvary Cemetery, with privilege to erect a headstone thereon.
"D. Brennan,
Supt. of Office of Calvary Cemetery.
"Grave 9, Plot F, Section 8, Range 56."

The title to the soil of Roman Catholic cemeteries is in the Bishop of the Catholic Church, in trust for the congregations and societies of the church under him, to be by them used and enjoyed according to the principles and polity of that church, to be used exclusively for the interment of those who at the time of their death were in regular standing in that church, according to its principles, usages, and doctrines; it being consecrated by religious services to that use; and according to its rules a permit must first be granted by the pastor of the church. The lot owner is bound by such doctrines and policies of the church, if he knows of them, and agrees to them, etc.[3] But

[1] *Dwenger et al. v. Geary et al.*, 113 Ind. 106 (1887); *Partridge et al. v. First Independent Church of Baltimore*, 39 Md. 631 (1873); *Rayner v. Nugent et al., adm'rs*, 60 Md. 515 (1883); *McGuire, adm'r, v. Trustees of St. Patrick's Cathedral*, 54 Hun (N. Y.) 207 (1889); *Kincaid's Appeal*, 66 Pa. St. 411 (1870).

[2] *McGuire, adm'r, v. Trustees of St. Patrick's Cathedral*, 54 Hun (N. Y.) 207 (1889).

[3] *Dwenger et al. v. Geary et al.*, 113 Ind. 106 (1887).

none but the church itself can rightfully declare who is a Catholic, it being a question of church government and discipline, and must be determined by the ecclesiastical authorities; and their decision is final.[1] A person who, having a sane mind, commits suicide, is never allowed knowingly to be interred in a Catholic cemetery.[2] In Canada an attempt was unsuccessfully made to refuse burial to a member of the "Institut Canadien," a literary society which had incurred ecclesiastical censure, the Bishop of Montreal having in his lifetime forbidden such membership on pain of being deprived of the sacrament.[3]

It is probably true that any organization, religious or secular, may control the right of burial in its own cemetery, and declare who shall enjoy it; and that liberty must be exercised so as not to encroach upon prior rights of others, but binds those who obtain privileges after such rights are acquired, taking subject to them. To hold otherwise would leave every possessor of a lot the privilege to do as he liked, and inter whom he pleased, however much his act might disturb the consciences of others. All that a lot owner acquires in a Catholic cemetery is a privilege to use it for the purpose to which it was dedicated, and the rules in force when he acquires such privilege measure the extent of, and limit, that use.[4]

---

[1] *White Lick Quarterly Meeting, &c.* v. *White Lick Quarterly Meeting, &c.*, 89 Ind. 136 (1883); *Dwenger et al.* v. *Geary et al.*, 113 Ind. 106 (1887); *McGuire, adm'r,* v. *Trustees of St. Patrick's Cathedral*, 54 Hun (N. Y.) 207 (1889).

[2] *Dwenger et al.* v. *Geary et al.*, 113 Ind. 106 (1887).

[3] *Brown* v. *Curé, &c. of Montreal*, L. R. 6 P. C. App. (Eng.) 157 (1874).

[4] *Dwenger et al.* v. *Geary et al.*, 113 Ind. 106 (1887).

Duration of Tenure. — A license to bury in the Catholic cemeteries may be revoked upon the licensee's becoming anti-Catholic, and equity will not aid in preventing the same.[1] In the case of *McGuire, adm'r, v. Trustees of St. Patrick's Cathedral*,[1] when the license was obtained the purchaser was a Catholic, but before he died he had apparently opposed the faith, and was not recognized as a Catholic by the church. The permit to bury was refused, though the wife of the deceased had been buried in the lot. Justice Daniels dissented from the rest of the court, holding that no evidence of any act on the part of the deceased that was scandalous or sinful had been introduced, that he had died in the faith of the Catholic Church, and that the permit ought not to be refused without giving the lot owner a chance to be heard.

The right to inter bodies in lots in cemeteries, be it an easement or a license, cannot continue longer than the territory is used as a cemetery,[2] or the corporation decide that the ground is no longer desirable as a place of interment, and the license is revoked, the right of future interment being thus extinguished.[3] So of the burying ground of a church.[4]

Interest in Proceeds of Sales of Lots. — Where a town cemetery is discontinued, lots in a new cemetery being given to owners of lots in the old one, and the bodies,

---

[1] *McGuire, adm'r, v. Trustees of St. Patrick's Cathedral*, 54 Hun (N. Y.) 207 (1889).

[2] *Page v. Symonds et al.*, 63 N. H. 17 (1883); *Kincaid's Appeal*, 66 Pa. St. 411 (1870).

[3] *Rayner v. Nugent et al., adm'rs*, 60 Md. 515 (1883).

[4] *Kincaid's Appeal*, 66 Pa. St. 411 (1870).

monuments, etc. removed, and the town voted that "all money received from the sale of lots," etc., "shall constitute a fund for the purpose of defraying the expense of repairing and improving the avenues, walks, and public grounds of the cemetery," there is no contract with the lot owners that the money received from that source shall be applied to the use and improvement of the cemetery, nor that the fund shall be set apart as a trust fund.[1]

Duty to Others. — Every right in a cemetery lot, from an absolute ownership to an easement and license, is held subject to the restriction that it shall not be so exercised as to injure others.[2]

Rights of the Public. — Lots are always held subject to the right of the public to take them for its own use if public necessity requires,[3] or when the abolition of the burial ground is necessary for sanitary reasons."[4]

Rules and regulations of the public burial board control lot owners in the use of their lots.[5]

Removal of Bodies on Abolition of Cemetery. — When it becomes necessary to vacate the ground for burial purposes, all that the lot holder can claim is notice of such vacation, that he may remove the bodies interred therein, and also the monuments, gravestones, etc., which he has placed thereon.[6] That is his only

[1] *Fay et al. v. Inhabitants of Milford*, 124 Mass. 79 (1878).
[2] *Kincaid's Appeal*, 66 Pa. St. 411 (1870).
[3] *Page v. Symonds et al.*, 63 N. H. 17 (1883).
[4] *Kincaid's Appeal*, 66 Pa. St. 411 (1870).
[5] *McGough v. Lancaster Burial Board*, L. R. 21 Q. B. Div. (Eng.) 323 (1888).
[6] *Partridge et al. v. First Independent Church of Baltimore*, 39 Md. 631 (1873); *Kincaid's Appeal*, 66 Pa. St. 411 (1870).

remaining right, and after that is exercised his interest and right therein absolutely cease.[1] On his failure to make such removal, others interested in the abolition of the cemetery can do so at their own expense.[2] The expense of removal, when it is done by the lot owner himself, can be collected of the parties in whose interest the abolition is made.[2] But he cannot claim compensation for monuments, vaults, etc., if he permits them to remain.[3] He can have no claim for reimbursement of the amount he paid for his right, whether he has ever used the lot for interments or not.[4]

Interest in the Rest of the Cemetery. — Lot owners and owners of graves have no control or rights in the remainder of the cemetery, except rights of way and such rights as are had by the public.[5]

If a corporation fails to keep the walks, drives, and approaches of its cemetery in proper repair, a lot owner can compel it to do so by a bill in equity.[6]

Where a lot is sold with reference to a plan, on which appears a certain avenue leading to or close beside the lot, affording a convenient highway to and from it, the purchaser has a right of way over it, and

---

[1] *Rayner* v. *Nugent et al., adm'rs*, 60 Md. 515 (1883).

[2] *Kincaid's Appeal*, 66 Pa. St. 411 (1870).

[3] *Partridge et al.* v. *First Independent Church of Baltimore*, 39 Md. 631 (1873).

[4] *Rayner* v. *Nugent et al., adm'rs*, 60 Md. 515 (1883); *Kincaid's Appeal*, 66 Pa. St. 411 (1870).

[5] *Moreland et al.* v. *Richardson et al.*, 22 Beav. (Eng.) 596 (1856); *Seymour* v. *Page*, 33 Conn. 61 (1865); *Price et al.* v. *M. E. Church et al.*, 4 Ohio 515 (1831).

[6] *Houston Cemetery Co. et al.* v. *Drew et al.*, 36 S. W. Rep. (Texas) 802 (1896).

it cannot be legally obstructed. Equity will protect this right by injunction if necessary, whether the lot owner has an absolute or a qualified interest in the lot.[1]

Privileges of Visitors. — Persons visiting the graves of deceased relatives or friends for the purpose of testifying their respect or affection for the dead have a right to do so, and, if they are improperly interfered with by the owner of the easement, a court of equity will interfere for their protection.[2]

Right to build Vaults and Tombs. — Every owner of a cemetery lot or other interest in a burial place, having the right to erect and maintain vaults for the purposes of interment, is subject to the police power of the State, in the exercise of which future interments may be prohibited and remains of persons already buried caused to be removed; and the power may be delegated to municipal corporations, and enforced by appropriate ordinances.[3] No conditions or covenants in deeds can prevent the legislature from declaring such use unlawful and causing its abandonment.[4]

In the case of *Rosehill Cemetery Co.* v. *Hopkinson, ex'x*,[5] the cemetery company had a rule that no vault or tomb should " be constructed in the cemetery until

---

[1] *Burke* v. *Wall et al.*, 29 La. Ann. 38 (1877). This servitude may be shown orally.

[2] *Smiley et al.* v. *Bartlett et al.*, 6 Ohio C. C. 234 (1892).

[3] *Page* v. *Symonds et al.*, 63 N. H. 17 (1883); *Went* v. *M. P. Church of Williamsburgh et al.*, 80 Hun (N. Y.) 266 (1894); *Humphrey et al.* v. *Trustees of M. E. Church*, 109 N. C. 132 (1891).

[4] *Went* v. *M. P. Church of Williamsburgh et al.*, 80 Hun (N. Y.) 266 (1894).

[5] *Rosehill Cemetery Co.* v. *Hopkinson, ex'x*, 114 Ill. 209 (1885).

the designs of the same accompanying the specifications, and a diagram of location, shall have been submitted to the board of managers, and approved by them"; and the deed of the lot in question was drawn subject to the act of incorporation and the rules and regulations thereto annexed, etc., one of the rules annexed being as follows: "The proprietor of each lot shall have the right to erect any proper stone or monument or sepulchral structure therein, except that no vault shall be built entirely above ground without permission of the company, and no monument and no portion of vaults above ground shall be of other material than cut stone, granite, or marble, without the consent of the company." The owner of the lot proceeded to erect a vault upon it, when the cemetery officers prevented further work. The vault was in itself satisfactory to the board of managers, but they objected to having a vault built on that particular lot, as it was in front of the entrance, and would somewhat obstruct the view. The court granted the prayer of a bill for an injunction against the interference of the cemetery corporation.

Interest in Associations. — Where the charter of an incorporated association provides that the members thereof numbering from five to fifteen, for instance, shall be elected by the association, lot owners do not become members until they are so elected,[1] and have no right to inspect the books of the company.[2]

Where an unincorporated association owns a burial

---

[1] *Bourland v. Springdale Cemetery Association*, 42 N. E. Rep. (Ill.) 86 (1895).

[2] *Bourland et al. v. Springdale Cemetery Association*, 56 Ill. App. 298 (1894).

ground, and provides that, if members withdraw, they shall " have no more right or title or interest in the aforesaid society, or interest in the benefit arising from the graveyard of the said society," it is not meant that a member owning a lot in the cemetery, in which he has made interments of persons in his family, loses all rights of burial in said lot, but is confined to the interest of the association in the income from the sale of lots, etc. in the cemetery. The owner of the lot acquires the privilege and right of making interments in the lot to the exclusion of others, so long as the ground remains a cemetery, and could maintain trespass *quare clausum fregit* for breaking and entering the same by digging a grave therein, in which the defendant buried the remains of a person without the consent of the plaintiff, who is the owner of the lot. And where malice or want of good faith is shown, the plaintiff is entitled to punitive damages.[1]

Rights in Free Cemeteries. — In a free neighborhood cemetery, when one has staked out a lot and entered into possession of it, and has not abandoned it, it is trespass in another to fence a part of this lot into his own lot, or to obstruct a roadway necessary for its use; and the possessor of the lot can defend his possession against such appropriation by his neighbor.[2] A cemetery corporation is liable also to the proprietor of a grave for the negligent burial of a stranger therein.[3] Where a man bought a lot in a cemetery of

---

[1] *Smith v. Thompson*, 55 Md. 5 (1880).

[2] *Pierce v. Spafford*, 53 Vt. 394 (1881).

[3] *Donnelly v. Boston Catholic Cemetery Association*, 146 Mass. 163 (1888).

a city and interred his child therein, the city having, through the agency of the sexton, the sole control and supervision of the cemetery, and the city subsequently wrongfully sold the lot to another person, the sexton carefully removing and reinterring the remains in a common burial lot, not knowing that the lot belonged to the father of the dead child, judgment was given against the city in a civil action brought for the trespass, the damages being merely nominal.[1]

Ornamentation. — The owners of lots or graves have a right to ornament them with shrubs and flowers;[2] and where a lot owner is given this right in the deed of the lot, he does not lose it by a rule or regulation of the cemetery association that he cannot have the work of ornamentation performed by others than himself and the cemetery employees, passed subsequently to the delivery of the deed.[3]

Recovery of Possession. — If a lot owner is ousted of his possession, his title to the lot and right of possession as licensee is insufficient to support an action of ejectment, the cemetery company having the possession legally.[4]

Construction of Deeds as to Bounds. — The deed of a lot owner which bounds his lot on an avenue does not convey any title to the middle of the avenue, as it would in ordinary conveyances. His right is only that which all the lot owners have, — a right of passage simply.[5] If the right of way to and from a

---

[1] *Hamilton* v. *City of New Albany*, 30 Ind. 482 (1868).

[2] *Ashby* v. *Harris*, L. R. 3 C. P. (Eng.) 523 (1868); *Commonwealth* v. *Viall*, 2 Allen (Mass.) 512 (1861).

[3] *Silverwood* v. *Latrobe et al.*, 68 Md. 620 (1888).

[4] *Hancock* v. *McAvoy*, 151 Pa. St. 460 (1892).

[5] *Seymour* v. *Page*, 33 Conn. 61 (1865).

lot is not disturbed, and the owner is not injured thereby, a cemetery association, acting in good faith, can close up an avenue and an open space adjoining the lot, and apply it to purposes beautifying the grounds, in spite of the objection of the lot owner.[1] These rights of the general owners of the cemetery are necessary in order to secure uniform taste and skill in the arrangement and care of the cemetery, and permanence and progress.[2]

Rights of Several Owners of Lots. — The purchase and use of a burial lot by several parties almost always cause disagreements and contests, and a state of things to be avoided. The only case of this kind of any importance is that of *Lewis* v. *Walker's ex'rs*.[3] In this case four brothers bought a burial lot, and divided its area among themselves. In the middle of the entire lot they erected at their joint expense a monument, on each side of which they inscribed the name of one of the brothers, and set apart the space opposite each name for such brother's family. In such a case, no one of the brothers can permit the interment in his portion of any person who is not a member of the family without the consent of the other brothers; and if the executors of the widow of one of the brothers cut off the raised letters on the face of the monument next her deceased husband's portion of the lot, leaving a smooth level surface, equity will not require an entirely new monument to be erected.

[1] *Perkins* v. *City of Lawrence*, 138 Mass. 361 (1885).
[2] *Seymour* v. *Page*, 33 Conn. 61 (1865).
[3] *Lewis* v. *Walker's ex'rs*, 165 Pa. St. 30 (1894).

CHAPTER XXV.

REPLEVIN.

THERE is no property nor right of property in a coffin or shroud after burial sufficient to support an action of replevin. So that proceeding cannot be used to recover a coffin and its contents, especially when such contents are a corpse. Articles after burial are a portion of the earth itself, in the eye of the law, whether they have begun to decay or not, provided they are deposited in the ground with the consent of those who had any pecuniary interest in them, and for the purpose of interment. They are no longer articles of merchandise, nor the property of those who furnished them. If replevin would lie in such cases, how many petty disputes would arise compelling the tomb to be unearthed, and all the sacredness surrounding our friends' remains and their last resting place to be at the mercilessness of any one who would swear that he was entitled to the possession of a shroud, or of some petty article buried with the body. The question of ownership could not be tried and determined until the desecration was complete. Such things must not be.[1] The case of *Guthrie* v. *Weaver*[1] was one where a sheriff, being possessed

---

[1] *Guthrie* v. *Weaver*, 1 Mo. App. 136 (1876).

of a replevin writ authorizing him to take a certain coffin, opened the grave, and took the coffin with the remains therein, to hold the same until the question of the title to the coffin — and body too, for that matter — should be determined in the courts of law. The court used exceedingly strong language against such a practice, saying that "no civilized community would endure such a rule of law as this."

CHAPTER XXVI.

LARCENY.

A CORPSE cannot be stolen at common law, as it is not property; but articles buried with it, which were merchandise before the interment, are also subjects of larceny after burial. These articles are the coffin, grave clothes, etc. In an indictment therefor they should be alleged to be the property of the person who furnished them and buried the deceased.[1]

It is larceny to take articles of dress from the body of a drowned man with the intention of stealing them; and in such a case the articles may be alleged in the indictment to be the property of the administrator of the estate of the deceased, though no administrator has been appointed.[2]

It is also a misdemeanor at common law to attempt to commit such larceny.[3]

To determine the degree of the crime, whether petty or grand larceny, the value of the articles is what is reasonable as to their cost in the market.[3]

---

[1] *Haynes' Case*, 12 Coke (Eng.) 113 (1614); *State* v. *Doepke*, 68 Mo. 208 (1878). In *Haynes' Case*, one William Haynes dug up the bodies of three men and one woman in one night, took off their winding sheets, and reinterred the remains.

[2] *Wonson* v. *Sayward*, 13 Pick. (Mass.) 402 (1832).

[3] *State* v. *Doepke*, 68 Mo. 208 (1878).

CHAPTER XXVII.

DESECRATION OF CEMETERIES.

The last resting places of the dead are regarded in a certain sense as sacred. They are universally considered as being hallowed. No one, other than the owners of the soil and those who have easements or other rights therein, has a right to, or can with impunity, disturb the soil, or anything in it or attached to it. Both the civil and criminal branches of the law, as well as equity, rise to their protection; and even attempts to injure or in any way desecrate such places are punished, and the guilty parties prohibited from carrying out their designs.

The Soil. — All suits for the disturbance of the soil can be brought by its general owners. If the soil is that of English churchyards, they must be in the name of the parson, of cemetery associations in their corporate name, of public cemeteries in the name of the town or city owning them, of denominational cemeteries in the name of the church, and of private cemeteries in the names of the owners of them, as the freehold, which is the tenure disturbed, is in these several parties only. An action generally lies in favor of either the owners of the freehold or the owners of the easement of burial, or both, when both have been injured, though it was early held in England that for the disturbance of human remains in churchyards only the parson had a right of action, the right of the heir of the deceased in the easement apparently being overlooked.

Fixtures. — If gravestones or other things that have been placed on or attached to lots in cemeteries are injured or taken away in the lifetime of the person or persons who erected them, such person or persons must be the plaintiffs in suits for damages therefor at common law; but if those persons have died before the injury is wrought, all subsequent suits must be brought by the heir of the deceased, and not his executor or administrator.[1] The same is true of a bill for an injunction, when injury is threatened;[2] and if it is desired that the injunction should apply to the whole yard, all the parties having such interests must be joined.[3] The reason of these rules is that those who erect monuments, etc., have a greater interest in their preservation than any other person, and this interest the law aims to protect. No one is so likely to care for them after their erectors have passed away as the descendants or heirs of those whose memory they preserve, and to them the law gives the right

---

[1] *Day* v. *Beddingfield et al.*, Noy (Eng.) 104 (1637); *Spooner* v. *Brewster*, 3 Bing. (Eng.) 136 (1825); *Sabin et al., ex'rs,* v. *Harkness*, 4 N. H. 415 (1828); *Matter of Brick Presbyterian Church*, 3 Edw. Ch. (N. Y.) 155 (1837); *Mitchell et al.* v. *Thorne*, 134 N. Y. 536 (1892); *Pierce et ux.* v. *Proprietors of Swan Point Cemetery et al.*, 10 R. I. 227 (1872).

[2] *Mitchell et al.* v. *Thorne*, 134 N. Y. 536 (1892).

[3] *Moreland et al.* v. *Richardson et al.*, 22 Beav. (Eng.) 596 (1856).

of action.[1] The fact that the ancestor died intestate makes no difference.[2]

Private Cemeteries. — In the case of *Mitchell et al. v. Thorne*,[2] a private burial place on the ancestor's own land, with a right of way thereto, was reserved to him and his heirs forever in a deed of the premises. The defendant, who held the estate under the grantee, proceeded to level off the graves, tear down the headstones, and destroy the enclosing fence, and threatened to continue the desecration. One of the heirs of the deceased original grantor brought suit for damages, and for an injunction restraining the threatened desecration. The court sustained the bill, and held that the fact that whether the ancestor had died testate or intestate had no effect upon the case, and that the fact of intestacy need not be stated in the bill.

Public Cemeteries. — In the case of *Commonwealth v. Viall*,[3] an ancient burial ground had been pastured by the owner of the fee, and otherwise treated as his own, except that he did not disturb the graves or their fixtures. It was taken by the town as a public cemetery, and subsequently he undertook to cut down some of the trees and cultivate a portion of the ground, but was restrained by the court from further demolition or use as the owner of the title to the soil.

Practice. — As the law can give only pecuniary damages for the desecration of a burial place, it is

---

[1] *Sabin et al., ex'rs, v. Harkness*, 4 N. H. 415 (1828); *Matter of Brick Presbyterian Church*, 3 Edw. Ch. (N. Y.) 155 (1837); *Mitchell et al. v. Thorne*, 57 Hun (N. Y.) 405 (1890).

[2] *Mitchell et al. v. Thorne*, 57 Hun (N. Y.) 405 (1890).

[3] *Commonwealth v. Viall*, 2 Allen (Mass.) 512 (1861).

inadequate as a means of protection. The equity court should be sought, and an injunction obtained to stop further desecration without delay.

In a civil action brought by an heir for the desecration of a cemetery lot for the recovery of damages, it is not necessary that all other parties having interests similar to that of the plaintiff should join with him, as he can only recover to the extent of his individual damage.[1]

Relatives or friends of the deceased persons buried there may enjoin the owner of the fee of a cemetery from desecrating their graves, or meddling with the monuments, etc., and all parties interested need not be joined as plaintiffs.[2]

The form of the action to be brought at law for damages is trespass, and not case.[3]

Where a cemetery is unnecessarily described, in an indictment for desecrating and disfiguring it, by metes and bounds, with minuteness and particularity, it must be proved exactly as set forth.[4]

[1] *Mitchell et al.* v. *Thorne*, 57 Hun (N. Y.) 405 (1890).
[2] *Davidson* v. *Reed et al.*, 111 Ill. 167 (1884).
[3] *Spooner* v. *Brewster*, 2 C. & P. (Eng.) 34 (1825).
[4] *Commonwealth* v. *Wellington*, 7 Allen (Mass.) 299 (1863).

CHAPTER XXVIII.

OPENING HIGHWAYS THROUGH CEMETERIES.

Ground consecrated for burial purposes cannot be applied to secular uses, nor the bodies of the dead buried therein removed by the owners of the soil without the authority of a legislative act at common law.[1]

In the United States it is generally held that the simple fact that lands have been previously devoted to cemetery purposes does not place them beyond the reach of the power of the principle of eminent domain.[2] And lands obtained by legal proceedings under the right of eminent domain, and also by purchase and conveyance from the owner, are both held in the same tenure in this respect. The general power which towns and cities have to take lands for public roads and streets is insufficient to enable them to condemn cemeteries, or any part of them, to such purposes. Such authority must be specially granted by the legislature, or necessarily and reasonably implied. But where the authority rests upon implication, it will be presumed that the legislature did not

---

[1] *Queen* v. *Twiss, Judge,* 10 B. & S. (Eng.) 298 (1869).

[2] *Board of Street Opening, &c.* v. *St. John's Cemetery,* 133 N. Y. 329 (1892).

so intend, unless there is a clear public necessity for the taking.[1]

These rules apply to every part of cemetery lands, whether they are occupied by graves or specially improved for such purposes or not, when statutes provide that no highways shall be laid through cemetery grounds.[2] But when a city dedicates a tract of land to cemetery purposes, and sells lots in the available parts of it, the city can subsequently to improvements being made by the purchasers of such lots permit a railroad to run through the unavailable portion, even against the protest of the lot owners.[3]

When land is taken from a cemetery against the will of the proprietors, the damages are the actual cash market value of the portion taken, in addition to the damages to the remainder which will be caused by both the construction and operation of the railroad; or the difference between the fair market value of the whole at the time of the taking and the fair market value of what remains after the taking.[4]

If a town insists upon its right to enter a cemetery and open a highway through it, relief can be sought in equity by injunction. Law is too feeble and slow a remedy, when a few hours' delay may result in

[1] *Evergreen Cemetery Association* v. *City of New Haven*, 43 Conn. 234 (1875).

[2] *Village of Hyde Park* v. *Oakwoods Cemetery Association*, 119 Ill. 141 (1886).

[3] *Wood et al.* v. *Macon and Brunswick R. R. Co. et al.*, 68 Ga. 539 (1882).

[4] *Concordia Cemetery Association* v. *Minnesota and Northwestern R. R. Co.*, 121 Ill. 199 (1887).

irreparable havoc among the gravestones, the mounds, and even the remains of loved ones.[1]

Though municipalities have no right of themselves to open streets through cemeteries, on the other hand a cemetery company has no authority to close an alley already opened because it has purchased ground on both sides of it.[2]

---

[1] *Trustees of First Evangelical Church et al.* v. *Walsh et al.*, 57 Ill. 363 (1870).

[2] *Du Bois Cemetery Co.* v. *Griffin et al.*, 165 Pa. St. 81 (1895).

CHAPTER XXIX.

ABOLITION OF CEMETERIES.

CEMETERIES are abolished in two ways, by abandonment and by an act of the legislature.

Abandonment. — Bodies are not buried for a certain period, but presumably for all time; and a cemetery therefore does not become legally abandoned by merely not making new interments therein, though a long period of time — sixty years, for instance — has elapsed, if it has once acquired the character of a cemetery.[1] But when all parties in interest appropriate the burial ground to other uses and purposes, or allow it to be destroyed or lose its identity as a burial place, and no longer regard it as such, it is a legal abandonment at common law. There must be an actual abandonment, as well as an intention to abandon.[2]

In the case of *Stevens* v. *Town of Norfolk*,[2] a town legally took certain land for the enlargement of their cemetery, and the title had become vested in the town

---

[1] *Commonwealth* v. *Wellington*, 7 Allen (Mass.) 299 (1863); *Campbell* v. *City of Kansas*, 102 Mo. 326 (1890); *Attorney General et al.* v. *Mayor, &c. of City of Newark*, 42 N. J. Eq. 531 (1887).

[2] *Stevens* v. *Town of Norfolk*, 42 Conn. 377 (1875).

for that use. But before any use had been made of it, at the instance of the owner, the town appointed a committee to procure another lot, and instructed the selectmen to convey back the land already taken. Another lot was purchased, but, as it proved unsuitable, and the selectmen declined to release the lot first taken to the owner, and the town instructed the committee later to proceed to occupy, lay out, and enclose the lot first taken, and subsequently voted to rescind the prior vote to release it, the vote to release was at the most only a declaration of an intention to abandon the land if another suitable lot should be obtained, although the value of the land had been deposited by the town with the treasurer of the county for the owner, according to law, and he had never taken it. Where a city takes possession of an ancient neighborhood burial ground, it cannot abandon it.[1]

Act of the Legislature. — The legislature has authority to confer upon a city the power to condemn a cemetery for park purposes.[2] Nothing but the most pressing public necessity should ever cause the rest and peace of the dead to be disturbed.[3] In the case of *Campbell* v. *City of Kansas*,[4] the city passed an ordinance in 1857 vacating land that had been dedicated to the public for burial purposes ten years previously, and prohibited further interments therein under a penalty, notifying by newspaper advertisement the

---

[1] *Campbell* v. *City of Kansas*, 102 Mo. 326 (1890).

[2] *Campbell* v. *City of Kansas*, 102 Mo. 326 (1890); *St. John's Cemetery*, 62 Hun (N. Y.) 499 (1891).

[3] *Campbell* v. *City of Kansas*, 102 Mo. 326 (1890); *Craig et al.* v. *First Presbyterian Church of Pittsburgh*, 88 Pa. St. 42 (1878).

[4] *Campbell* v. *City of Kansas*, 102 Mo. 326 (1890).

relatives of the persons buried there to remove their remains, which was done. The city then took exclusive possession, graded streets surrounding it, and used the land for breaking stone, etc., and subsequently converted it into a park, no objection being made by the people.

Where certain lands are vested, if vested at all, in trust merely for and subject to use as a burial ground forever, such use is perpetual, and the city authorities cannot, under statutory authority even, destroy it, and devote the land to other purposes, for the original use is not subject to legislative revocation, and therefore the statute authorizing such destruction is unconstitutional. Such is the strong position which the New Jersey court takes in the case of *Attorney General et al.* v. *Mayor, &c. of City of Newark*.[1] And the New York court holds that lot owners cannot be deprived of their property without their consent, if they have the title to the land, and that a direction by the legislature to the cemetery association having general charge of the cemetery to sell and convey it has no valid force.[2]

But under the application of the police power of the State all cemeteries can be abolished in proper cases; and the State can exercise this power either directly or by delegation to municipalities.[3] Injury to public

---

[1] *Attorney General et al.* v. *Mayor, &c. of City of Newark*, 42 N. J. Eq. 531 (1887).

[2] *Went* v. *M. P. Church of Williamsburgh et al.*, 80 Hun (N. Y.) 266 (1894).

[3] *Campbell* v. *City of Kansas*, 102 Mo. 326 (1890); *Craig et al.* v. *First Presbyterian Church of Pittsburgh*, 88 Pa. St. 42 (1878).

health must be the ruling cause of such abolition.[1] This may be done in view of the advance of urban population, if it is detrimental to public health or in danger of becoming so.[2] But a burial place does not become unsuitable for the purposes of interment because it hinders the improvement of the property in its vicinity, nor because the sight of it may produce in some persons disagreeable feelings.[3]

The abolition of burial grounds may be accomplished in two ways, — by prohibiting interments and permitting the bodies to remain in the ground, which is to be undisturbed in the future, and by prohibiting future interments and removing the remains to other cemeteries.[4] Prohibition of future burials simply destroys the rights of the public generally in the cemetery, says the court in the case of *Campbell* v. *City of Kansas*.[5] In the case of *Coates* v. *Mayor, &c. of City of New York*,[6] a statute authorized the city of New York to make by-laws " for regulating, or, if they find it necessary, preventing, the interment of the dead " within the city, and a by-law was passed prohibiting burials in certain portions of the city, under a penalty. Interments continued to be made in those portions, however, by persons having a right under grants of or

---

[1] *Campbell* v. *City of Kansas*, 102 Mo. 326 (1890); *Went* v. *M. P. Church of Williamsburgh et al.*, 80 Hun (N. Y.) 266 (1894).

[2] *Went* v. *M. P. Church of Williamsburgh et al.*, 80 Hun (N. Y.) 266 (1894).

[3] *Reed et al.* v. *Stouffer et al.*, 56 Md. 236 (1881).

[4] *Craig et al.* v. *First Presbyterian Church of Pittsburgh*, 88 Pa. St. 42 (1878).

[5] *Campbell* v. *City of Kansas*, 102 Mo. 326 (1890).

[6] *Coates* v. *Mayor, &c. of City of New York*, 7 Cowen (N. Y.) 585 (1827).

titles to land held in trust for the sole purpose of interment, some of which had been used for that purpose for more than a hundred years, and to some of which certain fees for burial were incident, and belonged to the persons having the right of interment therein. The act was regarded as a police regulation, and was held valid and operative as to these interments, and also to rights claimed by individual vault owners, in whose behalf some of the interments were made.

The recital in a special act of the legislature that the continuance of a cemetery or tombs in a church is dangerous to the public health, and an order that the remains be removed, and no more interments made, cannot be objected to.[1]

The legislature, in directing the removal of the dead, must provide for the expense of such removal, and, while it may impose that expense upon the respective burial lots, or upon their owners, they must proceed by lawful methods.[2] Probably in no case should the expense be borne by the relatives of the deceased persons whose bodies are buried therein.[3]

The remains, and the monuments, etc., on the lot can be removed by the relatives of the persons buried therein, and if they do not attend to it after a general notice, it is the duty of the public authorities to perform the service,[4] and they will not be liable to the

---

[1] *Sohier et. al.* v. *Trinity Church et al.*, 109 Mass. 1 (1871).

[2] *Went* v. *M. P. Church of Williamsburgh et al.*, 80 Hun (N. Y.) 266 (1894).

[3] *St. John's Cemetery*, 62 Hun (N. Y.) 499 (1891).

[4] *Campbell* v. *City of Kansas*, 102 Mo. 326 (1890); *St. John's Cemetery*, 62 Hun (N. Y.) 499 (1891).

families of the deceased if they remove the bodies without their knowledge after such notice.[1]

Churchyards and cemeteries of religious societies are more transitory than others. Those who inter the remains of their friends or relatives in such burial places have no right or title, and they cannot prevent the sale of such a cemetery by the corporation and the removal of the remains interred therein, if done in a proper and legal manner. Payments of fees and charges for interments give no title to the land, the right being simply to have the bodies remain there until the burial place should be discontinued, and then to have them removed and properly deposited in a new place of sepulture.[2] In the case of *Windt et al. v. German Reformed Church*,[3] the court[4] said: "It is painful and deeply abhorrent to the sensibilities of our nature to have the remains of beloved friends and relatives disturbed in their last homes, and removed by rude and careless hands to a distant cemetery, not hallowed by any of the associations which encircle the consecrated ground where we have deposited them in sadness and in sorrow. I confess that I have not become so much of a philosopher as to regard the bodies of deceased friends as nothing more nor better than

---

[1] *Bessemer Land & Improvement Co* v. *Jenkins*, 18 So. Rep. (Ala.) 565 (1895).

[2] *Partridge et al.* v. *First Independent Church of Baltimore*, 39 Md. 631 (1873); *Windt et al.* v. *German Reformed Church*, 4 Sandf. Ch. (N. Y.) 471 (1847); *Richards* v. *Northwest Protestant Dutch Church*, 32 Barb. (N. Y.) 42 (1859); *Craig et al.* v. *First Presbyterian Church of Pittsburgh*, 88 Pa. St. 42 (1878).

[3] *Windt et al.* v. *German Reformed Church*, **4 Sandf. Ch.** (N. Y.) 471 (1847).

[4] Hon. Lewis H. Sandford, vice-chancellor.

the clods of the valley, and that my sympathies were strongly enlisted in behalf of these complainants vindicating the repose of their kindred. But I cannot shut my eyes to the clear light of the law as applicable to this case."

A church organization can be allowed to abolish so much of the churchyard as is necessary to enable them to erect a new church thereon, and may be ordered to remove the bodies buried therein.[1]

When a religious corporation has received a fee of the ground on which the church and graveyard are located, subject only to the keeping of the whole to pious uses, such corporation can grant any length of lease or a fee of portions of the ground for burials or vaults; and in the latter case the grantee will obtain a fee.[2] In the case of *Richards* v. *Northwest Protestant Dutch Church*,[3] it was held that, although such a lot was conveyed by deed to the grantee " and his heirs and assigns forever," stipulating that it shall "never be dug up, disturbed, or destroyed," yet, if it describes the premises as belonging to a church corporation, or adjacent to a church edifice, or in a churchyard, etc., it gives the right of interment in the particular plat of ground so long as that and the contiguous ground continues to be occupied as a churchyard. Every person taking a right takes it with knowledge that the conditions are liable to change.

---

[1] *Price et al.* v. *M. E. Church et al.*, 4 Ohio 515 (1831).

[2] *Matter of Brick Presbyterian Church*, 3 Edw. Ch. (N. Y.) 155 (1837); *Windt et al.* v. *German Reformed Church*, 4 Sandf. Ch. (N. Y.) 471 (1847).

[3] *Richards* v. *Northwest Protestant Dutch Church*, 32 Barb. (N. Y.) 42 (1859).

But where there is an actual legal fee conveyed, the property cannot be sold while such lot owner objects to the sale.[1] To enable one to raise the point that an act of the assembly authorizing the removal of the dead impairs the obligation of a contract, it is not sufficient to show that he has relatives interred in the grounds; he must prove by the record that he has rights of sepulture there, or some contract relation with the church.[2]

When church burial grounds are abolished the lot holders can claim no compensation or reimbursement out of the proceeds of the sale of the premises by the corporation, or for the improvements or erections (such as vaults, etc.) which he has placed thereon. In such cases all monuments and other structures capable of being removed are the personal property of the lot holder, and he can remove them upon the abolition of the cemetery.[3]

In an application to court by a religious organization for leave to sell its church and grounds, it is not necessary, probably, to state that they have found a purchaser, and fixed upon a new site. A conditional order may be made.[4]

Where grounds were conveyed to a certain congregation, and by it appropriated to burial purposes, the congregation having grown subsequently so much that

[1] *Matter of Brick Presbyterian Church*, 3 Edw. Ch. (N. Y.) 155 (1837).

[2] *Craig et al.* v. *First Presbyterian Church of Pittsburgh*, 88 Pa. St. 42 (1878).

[3] *Partridge et al.* v. *First Independent Church of Baltimore*, 39 Md. 631 (1873).

[4] *Matter of Brick Presbyterian Church*, 3 Edw. Ch. (N. Y.) 155 (1837).

it was divided into three, the ground was conveyed to the three as tenants in common equally, lots were sold to individuals, and interments made; and later an act of the assembly authorized the vacation and sale of the ground by commissioners, and the removal of the bodies to other lots to be purchased with the proceeds of the sale, and after payment of the expense the payment of the balance to the lot holders according to their respective interests, to be ascertained by the court, the congregation should be made parties to a bill by the lot holders to restrain the commissioners from carrying out the act of the assembly.[1]

[1] *Kincaid's Appeal*, 66 Pa. St. 411 (1870).

CHAPTER XXX.

JURISDICTION OF COURTS.

The jurisdiction of the courts in England in all mortuary matters is divided between the ecclesiastical and the law courts, but not so clearly but that contests concerning their respective jurisdictions frequently raged. The ecclesiastical courts have cognizance of all controversies relating to burials in consecrated ground.[1] This jurisdiction was confined to the mode of burial and the protection of the body, except that they could not affect property rights, nor the police powers of the State. The church first had charge of the remains of the great lights of its clergy, then of saints generally, and finally of all its parishioners. The bodies of the saints, both famed and unfamed, were held as sacred, and the law yielded the control and government of sacred things to the church, which is only a branch of the general authority and government of England. The church obtained this exclusive power, both executive and judicial, as well as legislative, soon after the Conquest.

Every man had the right to be buried in the churchyard of the parish where he lived,[2] but the parson

---

[1] *King* v. *Coleridge et al.*, 2 B. & Ald. (Eng.) 806 (1819).

[2] *Foster* v. *Dodd et al.*, 8 B. & S. (Eng.) 842 (1867); *Pierce et ux.* v. *Proprietors of Swan Point Cemetery et al.*, 10 R. I. 227 (1872).

could in many respects deal with it as if it were his private property.

It was held in the English case of *In re Rector, &c. of St. George-in-the-East*,[1] that the consistory court of London could empower the rector and church wardens on their petition to construct paths, etc. over and through a part of their churchyard which was closed to further burials, that it might be used for a public garden. The court, however, could not order that the cemetery be put to other uses.[2]

It was the Christian belief in the resurrection of the body that caused the burial of the dead to be taken in charge by the church. Connected with the exercise of that belief was a refusal of the rites of Christian burial to certain unregenerate persons, such as traitors, murderers, suicides, etc. For the disposition of the dead bodies of such persons the church made no provision. If left to the church alone, such would have perished like the beasts, with no human eye to see, and no human heart to pity, and no human hand to bestow upon that which was formed in the likeness of God the last act of common decency.

The civil courts of England have jurisdiction over the title to and possession of the grounds, monuments, etc., and of all actions of trespass, etc., and in the enforcement of the police powers of the State.

In America there are no ecclesiastical tribunals that the law recognizes. The questions that arise in mortuary matters are generally within the jurisdiction of the court of equity, though there are many cases in

---

[1] *In re Rector, &c. of St. George-in-the-East*, L. R 1 P. Div. (Eng.) 311 (1876).

[2] *Queen v. Twiss*, L. R. 4 Q. B. (Eng.) 407 (1869).

which legal remedies are amply sufficient.[1] For instance, the court of equity has power to enjoin boards of health of towns from establishing burial places, if they should proceed to do it illegally or improperly, to the injury of others.[2] Equity can always be sought in these matters, if it appears that the law is inadequate to give full redress, as in cases where relatives of the deceased have no standing in a law court because of lack of contractual relations, etc., with the owners of the cemeteries, and no right to complain under the strict rules of law.[3]

[1] *Weld* v. *Walker et al.*, 130 Mass. 422 (1881).
[2] *Upjohn* v. *Board of Health et al.*, 46 Mich. 542 (1881).
[3] *Boyce et al.* v. *Kalbaugh et al.*, 47 Md. 334 (1877).

INDEX.

	PAGE
ABANDONMENT OF CEMETERIES, effect of	199
ABOLITION OF CEMETERIES	199
by abandonment	199
by Act of Legislature	200
of religious societies	204
ACQUIREMENT OF LAND FOR CEMETERY PURPOSES	136
by conveyance	141
by dedication	137
by prescription	136
by right of eminent domain	142
AMOUNT ALLOWED FOR FUNERAL EXPENSES	70
monuments, etc.	89
APPLICATION TO TAKE LAND FOR CEMETERY PURPOSES BY RIGHT OF EMINENT DOMAIN	146
ASSOCIATIONS, CEMETERY	128
interest of lot owners in	185
ATTENDANCE OF SOCIETIES AT FUNERALS	
expense of	67
AUTOPSIES IN INQUESTS	16, 20
other cases	20
BEARERS, expense of	67
pall-bearers, expense of	67
BODIES, DEAD HUMAN	
custody of	26
disposition of	30

BODIES, DEAD HUMAN — *continued.*

	PAGE
laying out	62
property in	22, 23
sale of, for dissection	22
transportation of	62

BODY-SNATCHING 21, 22
BOUNDS AND FENCES OF BURIAL LOTS . . 99
BURIAL 41

duty of	36
record of	9
right of	30
permits	100

BURIAL LOT, expense of 68
BY-LAWS 159

municipal	159
of cemetery associations	161

CARE AND CONDUCT OF CEMETERIES . . . 172
CARRIAGES AT FUNERALS, expense of 67
CEMETERIES 114

what constitutes a cemetery	117
kinds	119
associations	128
churchyards	120
denominational	123
free	127
interments in churches	119
national	125
private	131
public	125
State	125
tombs	114
establishment of	119
acquirement of land for	136
care and conduct of	172
as charities	155
as nuisances	149
practice	154

INDEX.

CEMETERIES — *continued.*   PAGE
    desecration of 192
    opening highways through 196
    abolition of 199
    prohibition of 133
        of establishment 133
        of further use 134
CHARITIES, CEMETERIES AS 155
CHURCHES, INTERMENTS IN 119
CHURCHYARDS 120
COFFINS 53, 54, 63
CONVEYANCE OF THE RIGHT OF THE PUB-
    LIC IN DEDICATED CEMETERY LANDS . 140
CORONERS 13
    right of custody of certain dead bodies 28
COURTS, JURISDICTION OF 208
CREMATION 44
CUSTODY OF DEAD BODIES 26
    license to enter premises to take 26
    to whom custody belongs 26
    actions for deprivation of 28

DAMAGES FOR TAKING LANDS FOR CEME-
    TERY PURPOSES BY RIGHT OF EMINENT
    DOMAIN 146
DEATH
    notice of 62
    presumption of 7
    record of 9
DEDICATION, ACQUIREMENT OF CEMETERY
    LANDS BY 137
    effect of 140
    nature of right parted with 140
    time as an element of 140
DEEDS OF BURIAL LOTS, AS TO BOUNDS,
    CONSTRUCTION OF 187

INDEX.

	PAGE
DENOMINATIONAL CEMETERIES	123
rules of	161
DESECRATION OF CEMETERIES	192
of the soil	192
of the fixtures	193
private cemeteries	194
public cemeteries	194
practice	194
DISPOSITION OF DEAD BODIES	30
duty of	36
manner of	39
right of	30
DISSECTION	21, 46
sale of bodies for	22
DUTY OF BURIAL	36
of personal representatives	36
of relatives	37
of others	38, 39
EMBALMING	47
EMINENT DOMAIN, ACQUIREMENT OF CEMETERY LANDS BY RIGHT OF	142
purpose of the taking	142
necessity for the taking	144
who decides	146
application	146
damages	146
EPITAPHS ON MONUMENTS, ETC.	96
ESTABLISHMENT OF CEMETERIES	119
acquirement of lands	136
prohibition of	133
EXAMINATIONS, POST MORTEM	20
EXHUMATION OF DEAD BODIES	109
permits for	100, 102
EXPENSES	
of last sickness. See LAST SICKNESS.	
of inquests	17

EXPENSES — *continued.*

   of funerals 59
      gratuitous services 59
      notice of indebtedness 77
      who may contract therefor 73
      who are primarily liable 78
         where credit is given 83
      amount allowed 70
      practice 83
      what is included :
         laying out the body 62
         notice of death 62
         transportation of body 62
         shroud 63
         coffin 63
         wake 63
         funeral services 64
         refreshments 64
         mourning 64
         mourning rings 66
         gloves 66
         portrait 67
         bearers 67
         pall 67
         pall-bearers 67
         carriages 67
         attendance of societies at funerals 67
         burial lot 68
         grave 69
         marking place of interment 69
            monuments 86
         reinterment 70

FREE CEMETERIES 127
   rights of lot holders in 186

FUNERAL 51
   expenses 59
   services 52, 55, 56
   wakes 55
   pall 55

FUNERAL—*continued.*

	Page
mourning	57
refreshments	57
mourning rings	57
gloves	58

GLOVES 58
    expense of 66
GRATUITOUS SERVICES 59
GRAVE, EXPENSE OF DIGGING 69
GRAVESTONES. See Monuments.

HEARINGS, INQUEST 11–19
HIGHWAYS THROUGH CEMETERIES, OPENING 196

INQUESTS 11
    in what cases held 11
    information of death 12
    time of holding 12
    place of holding 13
    by whom held 13
    the hearing 14
    autopsy 16
    expenses 17
    interference with 19
    second 19
INSCRIPTIONS ON MONUMENTS, ETC. . . 96

JURISDICTION OF COURTS 208

KINDS OF CEMETERIES 119

LARCENY 191
LAST SICKNESS 1
    duration of 2
    character of service 4
    expense of 4
        who is responsible therefor 5
        amount allowed 6

INDEX.

	PAGE
LAYING OUT DEAD BODIES	62
LOT OWNERS, RIGHTS AND LIABILITIES OF	177
tenure	177
duration of	181
interest in proceeds of sales of lots	181
duty to others	182
rights of the public	182
interest in the remainder of the cemetery	183
privileges of visitors	184
interest in associations	185
rights in free cemeteries	186
ornamentation	187
right to build vaults and tombs	184
recovery of possession	187
removal of bodies on abolition of cemetery	182
construction of deeds as to bounds	187
rights of several owners of lots	188
MANNER OF DISPOSITION OF DEAD BODIES	39
burial	41, 52
cremation	44
dissection	46
embalming	47
MARKING PLACE OF INTERMENT, expense of	69
MONUMENTS	86
desires of deceased concerning, expressed orally	91
directions in wills	91
who can contract therefor	87
amount allowed to be expended therefor	89
inscriptions on	96
property in	99
allowance for two tombstones	95
exchange of	95
MORTGAGE OF CEMETERY PROPERTY	170
MORTUARIES	84
MOURNING	57
expense of	64

INDEX.

	PAGE
MOURNING RINGS	57
expense of	66
MUTILATION OF DEAD BODIES	20
dissection	21
NATIONAL CEMETERIES	125
NOTICE	
of death	62
of funeral expenditures	77
NUISANCES, CEMETERIES AS	149
ORDINANCES, MUNICIPAL	159
ORNAMENTATION OF CEMETERIES	187
PALL-BEARERS, expense of	67
PALLS	55
expense of	67
PARTIES TO BILLS FOR ABOLITION OF CEMETERIES AS NUISANCES	154
PARTITION OF CEMETERY PROPERTY	171
PERMITS TO TRANSPORT, BURY, AND EXHUME DEAD BODIES	100
PERSONAL REPRESENTATIVES	
duty of burial	36
right of burial	34
PORTRAIT OF DECEASED, expense of	67
PRACTICE	
concerning funeral expenses	83
desecration of cemeteries	194
quashing assessments for tax of cemetery property, etc.	168
recovery of possession of burial lot	187
who decides the purpose of necessity for taking lands for cemetery purposes by right of eminent domain	146
parties to bill for abolition of cemetery as a nuisance	154
PRESCRIPTION, ACQUIREMENT OF CEMETERY LANDS BY	136
PRESUMPTION OF DEATH	7

INDEX.

	PAGE
PRIVATE CEMETERIES	131
desecration of	194
PROHIBITION OF CEMETERIES	133
of establishment of	133
of further use of	134
PROPERTY	
in dead bodies	22, 23
in monuments, etc.	99
PUBLIC CEMETERIES	125
desecration of	194
RECORD OF DEATHS AND BURIALS	9
REFRESHMENTS AT FUNERALS	57
expense of	64
REINTERMENT	
right of	34
expense of	70
RELATIVES	
duty of burial	37
right of burial	32
REPLEVIN	189
REVERSION OF LANDS DEDICATED TO OR TAKEN BY RIGHT OF EMINENT DOMAIN FOR CEMETERY PURPOSES	147
RIGHT OF BURIAL	30
of the deceased	30
of relatives	32
of personal representatives	34
of reinterment	34
legal nature of	36
its termination	32
RULES AND REGULATIONS	159
for denominational cemeteries	161
SALE OF DEAD BODIES	22
SALE OF CEMETERY PROPERTY	169
on execution	169

	PAGE
SERVICES, FUNERAL	52, 55, 56, 59
gratuitous	59
expense of	64
SHROUD	63
SICKNESS, LAST. See LAST SICKNESS.	
SOCIETIES AT FUNERALS, EXPENSE OF ATTENDANCE OF	67
STATE CEMETERIES	125
TAXATION	162
what is meant by taxes	163
kind of property exempted from	164
what land is exempted from	164
who should be assessed for taxes	167
quashing assessment, etc.	168
effect of prohibition of interments	167
collection of taxes	167
TENURE OF OWNERS OF LOTS IN CEMETERIES	177
duration of	181
TOMBS	114
right of lot owners to build	184
TRANSPORTATION OF DEAD BODIES	62, 103
at common law	103
statutory provisions	104
permits for	100
UNDERTAKERS	48, 52
VAULTS, RIGHT OF LOT OWNERS TO BUILD	184
VISITORS TO CEMETERIES, PRIVILEGES OF	184
WAKES	55
expenses of	63